NIST Special Publication 800-175B
Revision 1

Guideline for Using Cryptographic Standards in the Federal Government:

Cryptographic Mechanisms

Elaine Barker

COMPUTER SECURITY

National Institute of
Standards and Technology
U.S. Department of Commerce

NIST Special Publication 800-175B
Revision 1

Guideline for Using Cryptographic Standards in the Federal Government:

Cryptographic Mechanisms

Elaine Barker
Computer Security Division
Information Technology Laboratory

March 2020

U.S. Department of Commerce
Wilbur L. Ross, Jr., Secretary

National Institute of Standards and Technology
Walter Copan, Director of NIST and Under Secretary of Commerce for Standards and Technology

Authority

This publication has been developed by NIST in accordance with its statutory responsibilities under the Federal Information Security Modernization Act (FISMA) of 2014, 44 U.S.C. § 3551 *et seq.*, Public Law (P.L.) 113-283. NIST is responsible for developing information security standards and guidelines, including minimum requirements for federal information systems, but such standards and guidelines shall not apply to national security systems without the express approval of appropriate federal officials exercising policy authority over such systems. This guideline is consistent with the requirements of the Office of Management and Budget (OMB) Circular A-130.

Nothing in this publication should be taken to contradict the standards and guidelines made mandatory and binding on federal agencies by the Secretary of Commerce under statutory authority. Nor should these guidelines be interpreted as altering or superseding the existing authorities of the Secretary of Commerce, Director of the OMB, or any other federal official. This publication may be used by nongovernmental organizations on a voluntary basis and is not subject to copyright in the United States. Attribution would, however, be appreciated by NIST.

National Institute of Standards and Technology Special Publication 800-175B Revision 1
Natl. Inst. Stand. Technol. Spec. Publ. 800-175B Rev. 1, 91 pages (March 2020)
CODEN: NSPUE2

Comments on this publication may be submitted to:

National Institute of Standards and Technology
Attn: Computer Security Division, Information Technology Laboratory
100 Bureau Drive (Mail Stop 8930) Gaithersburg, MD 20899-8930
Email: SP800-175@nist.gov

All comments are subject to release under the Freedom of Information Act (FOIA).

Reports on Computer Systems Technology

The Information Technology Laboratory (ITL) at the National Institute of Standards and Technology (NIST) promotes the U.S. economy and public welfare by providing technical leadership for the Nation's measurement and standards infrastructure. ITL develops tests, test methods, reference data, proof of concept implementations, and technical analyses to advance the development and productive use of information technology. ITL's responsibilities include the development of management, administrative, technical, and physical standards and guidelines for the cost-effective security and privacy of other than national security-related information in federal information systems. The Special Publication 800-series reports on ITL's research, guidelines, and outreach efforts in information system security, and its collaborative activities with industry, government, and academic organizations.

Abstract

This document provides guidance to the Federal Government for using cryptography and NIST's cryptographic standards to protect sensitive but unclassified digitized information during transmission and while in storage. The cryptographic methods and services to be used are discussed.

Keywords

asymmetric-key algorithm; identity authentication; confidentiality; digital signatures; encryption; integrity; key establishment; message authentication; random bit generation; symmetric-key algorithm.

Acknowledgments

The author wishes to thank the authors of SP 800-21[1] from which this document was derived, Annabelle Lee and William C. Barker, along with those colleagues that reviewed drafts of this document and contributed to its development: Lily Chen, Kerry McKay and Lydia Zieglar (NSA). The author also gratefully acknowledges and appreciates the many comments from the public and private sectors whose thoughtful and constructive comments improved the quality and usefulness of this publication.

---

[1] SP 800-21, *Guideline for Implementing Cryptography in the Federal Government.*

Patent Disclosure Notice

Table of Contents

List of Figures

1 Introduction

1.1 Overview and Purpose

In today's environment of increasingly open and interconnected systems, networks, and mobile devices, network and data security are essential for the optimal safe use of information technology. Cryptographic techniques should be considered for the protection of data that is sensitive, has a high value, or is vulnerable to unauthorized disclosure or undetected modification during transmission or while in storage.

Cryptography is a branch of mathematics that is based on the transformation of data and can be used to provide several security services: confidentiality, identity authentication, data integrity authentication, source authentication, and support for non-repudiation.

- *Confidentiality* is the property whereby sensitive information is not disclosed to unauthorized entities. A confidentiality service can be provided by a cryptographic process called *encryption*.

- *Data integrity authentication* (also called *integrity verification*) is a service that is used to determine that data has not been altered in an unauthorized manner since it was created, transmitted, or stored.

- *Identity authentication* is used to provide assurance of the identity of an entity interacting with a system.

- *Source authentication* is used to provide assurance of the source of information to a receiving entity (i.e., the identity of the source). A special case of source authentication is called *non-repudiation*, whereby support for assurance of the source of the information is provided to a third party.

This document is one part in a series of documents intended to provide guidance to the Federal Government for using cryptography to protect its sensitive but unclassified digitized information during transmission and while in storage; hereafter, the shortened term "sensitive" will be used to refer to this class of information. Other sectors are invited to use this guidance on a voluntary basis. The following are the initial publications in the Special Publication (SP) 800-175 series. Additional documents may be provided in the future.

- <u>SP 800-175A</u>[2] provides guidance on the determination of requirements for using cryptography. It includes the laws and regulations for the protection of the Federal Government's sensitive information, guidance for the conduct of risk assessments to determine what needs to be protected and how best to protect that information, and a discussion of the required security-related documents (e.g., various policy and practice documents).

---

[2] SP 800-175A, *Guideline for Using Cryptographic Standards in the Federal Government: Directives, Mandates and Policies.*

- SP 800-175B (this document) discusses the cryptographic methods and services available for the protection of the Federal Government's sensitive information and provides an overview of NIST's cryptographic standards.

1.2   Audience

This document is intended for federal employees and others who are responsible for providing and using cryptographic services to meet identified security requirements. This document might be used by

- A program manager responsible for selecting and integrating cryptographic mechanisms into a system;

- A technical specialist who has been requested to select one or more cryptographic methods/techniques to meet a specified requirement;

- A procurement specialist developing a solicitation for a system, network, or service that will require cryptographic methods to perform security functionality; and

- Users of cryptographic services.

The goal is to provide these individuals with sufficient information to allow them to make informed decisions about the cryptographic methods that will meet their specific needs to protect the confidentiality and integrity of data that is transmitted and/or stored in a system or network, as well as to obtain assurance of its authenticity.

This document is not intended to provide information on the federal procurement process or to provide a technical discussion on the mathematics of cryptography and cryptographic algorithms.

1.3   Scope

This document limits its scope of cryptographic methods to those that conform to Federal Information Processing Standards (FIPS) and NIST Special Publications (SPs), which are collectively discussed as NIST "standards" in this document. While the Federal Government is required to use these standards when applicable, industry, national, and international standards bodies have also adopted these cryptographic methods.

This document provides information on selecting and using cryptography in new or existing systems.

1.4   Background

The use of cryptography relies upon two basic components: an *algorithm* and a *key*. The algorithm is a mathematical function, and the key is a parameter used during the cryptographic process. The algorithm and key are used together to apply cryptographic protection to data (e.g., to encrypt the data or to generate a digital signature) and to remove or check the protection (e.g., to decrypt the encrypted data or to verify the digital signature). The security of the cryptographic protection relies on the secrecy of the key. Security should not rely on the secrecy of the algorithm as the algorithm specification may be publicly available.

In order to use a cryptographic algorithm, any required cryptographic keys must be "in place" (i.e., keys must be established for and/or between parties that intend to use cryptography). Keys may be established either manually (e.g., via a trusted courier) or using an automated method. However, when an automated method is used, source authentication is required for the participating entities that relies on an established trust infrastructure, such as a Public Key Infrastructure (PKI) or a manually distributed authentication key.

In general, keys used for one purpose (e.g., the generation of digital signatures) must not be used for another purpose (e.g., key establishment) because the use of the same key for two different cryptographic processes may weaken the security provided by one or both of the processes. See Section 5.2 in SP 800-57, Part 1[3] for further information.

1.5   Terms and Definitions

The following terms and definitions are used in this document. In general, the definitions are drawn from FIPS and NIST Special Publications.

Algorithm	A clearly specified mathematical process for computation; a set of rules that, if followed, will give a prescribed result.
Approved	FIPS-Approved and/or NIST-recommended. An algorithm or technique that is either: 1) specified in a FIPS or NIST Recommendation or 2) specified elsewhere and adopted by reference in a FIPS or NIST Recommendation.
Asymmetric-key algorithm	See *public-key algorithm*.
Authentication	A process that provides assurance of the source and integrity of information that is communicated or stored or the identity of an entity interacting with a system.
	Note that in common practice, the term "authentication" is used to mean either source or identity authentication only. This document will differentiate the multiple uses of the word by the terms source authentication, identity authentication, or integrity authentication, where appropriate.
Bit string	An ordered sequence of 0's and 1's.
Block cipher algorithm	A family of functions and their inverse functions that is parameterized by cryptographic keys; the functions map bit strings of a fixed length to bit strings of the same length.
Certificate (or public key certificate)	A set of data that uniquely identifies an entity, contains the entity's public key and possibly other information, and is

---

[3] SP 800-57 Part 1, *Recommendation for Key Management: General Guideline.*

digitally signed by a trusted party, thereby binding the public key to the entity identified in the certificate. Additional information in the certificate could specify how the key is used and the validity period of the certificate.

Certificate Revocation List (CRL)	A list of revoked but unexpired certificates issued by a Certification Authority.
Certification Authority (CA)	The entity in a public key infrastructure (PKI) that is responsible for issuing certificates to certificate subjects and exacting compliance to a PKI policy.
Ciphertext	Data in its encrypted form.
Compromise	The unauthorized disclosure, modification, substitution, or use of sensitive data (e.g., a secret key, private key, or secret metadata).
Confidentiality	The property that sensitive information is not disclosed to unauthorized entities (i.e., the secrecy of key information is maintained).
Cross-certify	The establishment of a trust relationship between two Certification Authorities (CAs) through the signing of each other's public key in certificates; referred to as a "cross-certificate."
Cryptographic algorithm	A well-defined computational procedure that takes variable inputs, including a cryptographic key (if applicable), and produces an output.
Cryptographic boundary	An explicitly defined continuous perimeter that establishes the physical bounds of a cryptographic module and contains all the hardware, software, and/or firmware components of a cryptographic module.
Cryptographic checksum	A mathematical value created using a cryptographic algorithm that is assigned to data and later used to test the data to verify that the data has not changed.
Cryptographic hash function	A function that maps a bit string of arbitrary length to a fixed-length bit string. **Approved** hash functions satisfy the following properties: 1. One-way – It is computationally infeasible to find any input that maps to any pre-specified output.

2. Collision resistant – It is computationally infeasible to find any two distinct inputs that map to the same output.

Cryptographic key	A parameter used in conjunction with a <u>cryptographic algorithm</u> that determines its operation in such a way that an <u>entity</u> with knowledge of the key can reproduce or reverse the operation while an entity without knowledge of the key cannot. Examples include 1. The transformation of <u>plaintext</u> data into <u>ciphertext</u> data, 2. The transformation of ciphertext data into plaintext data, 3. The computation of a <u>digital signature</u> from data, 4. The verification of a digital signature, 5. The computation of a <u>message authentication code</u> (MAC) from data, 6. The verification of a MAC received with data, 7. The computation of a <u>shared secret</u> that is used to derive <u>keying material.</u>
Cryptographic module	The set of hardware, software, and/or firmware that implements **approved** security functions (including <u>cryptographic algorithms</u> and <u>key</u> generation) and is contained within a <u>cryptographic boundary</u>.
Cryptographic primitive	A low-level <u>cryptographic algorithm</u> used as a basic building block for higher-level cryptographic algorithms.
Cryptography	The discipline that embodies the principles, means, and methods for providing information security, including <u>confidentiality</u>, <u>data integrity</u>, <u>source authentication</u>, and <u>non-repudiation</u>.
Cryptoperiod	The time span during which a specific <u>key</u> is authorized for use or in which the keys for a given system may remain in effect.
Data integrity	A property whereby data has not been altered in an unauthorized manner since it was created, transmitted, or stored.
Data integrity authentication	The process of determining the <u>integrity</u> of the data; also called <u>integrity authentication</u> or <u>integrity verification</u>.
Decryption	The process of changing <u>ciphertext</u> into <u>plaintext</u> using a <u>cryptographic algorithm</u> and <u>key</u>.
Digital signature	The result of a cryptographic transformation of data that, when properly implemented, provides the services of

1. Source authentication,

2. Data integrity, and

3. Support for signer non-repudiation.

Digital Signature Algorithm (DSA)	A public-key algorithm that is used for the generation and verification of digital signatures.
Domain parameters	The parameters used with a cryptographic algorithm that are common to a domain of users.
Elliptic Curve Digital Signature Algorithm (ECDSA)	A digital signature algorithm that is an analog of DSA using elliptic curves.
Encryption	The process of changing plaintext into ciphertext using a cryptographic algorithm for the purpose of security or privacy.
Entity	An individual (person), organization, device, or process.
Ephemeral key pair	A short-term key pair used with a public-key (asymmetric-key) algorithm that is generated when needed; the public key of an ephemeral key pair is not provided in a public key certificate, unlike static public keys which are often included in a certificate.
Function	Used interchangeably with algorithm in this document.
Hash function	See *cryptographic hash function*.
Hash value	The result of applying a hash function to information; also called a message digest.
Identity authentication	The process of providing assurance about the identity of an entity interacting with a system; also see Source authentication.
Initialization Vector (IV)	A vector used in defining the starting point of a cryptographic process.
Integrity	The property that data has not been modified or deleted in an unauthorized and undetected manner.
Integrity authentication (integrity verification)	The process of determining the integrity of the data; also called data integrity authentication.
Interoperability	The ability of one entity to communicate with another entity.
Key	See *cryptographic key*.

Key agreement	A (pair-wise) key-establishment procedure where secret keying material is generated from information contributed by two participants so that no party can predetermine the value of the secret keying material independently from the contributions of the other party. Contrast with key-transport.
Key confirmation	A procedure used to provide assurance to one party that another party actually possesses the same keying material and/or shared secret.
Key derivation	The process by which keying material is derived from either a pre-shared key or a shared secret produced during a key-agreement scheme along with other information.
Key establishment	The procedure that results in keying material that is shared among different entities.
Key information	Information about a key that includes the keying material and associated metadata relating to that key.
Key management	The activities involving the handling of cryptographic keys and other related security parameters (e.g., IVs and counters) during the entire life cycle of the keys, including their generation, storage, establishment, entry, output, use, and destruction.
Key pair	A public key and its corresponding private key; a key pair is used with a public-key (asymmetric-key) algorithm.
Key transport	A key-establishment procedure whereby one party (the sender) selects a value for the secret keying material and then securely distributes that value to another party (the receiver). Contrast with key agreement.
Key wrapping	A method of cryptographically protecting the confidentiality and integrity of keys using a symmetric-key algorithm.
Key-wrapping key	A symmetric key used to provide confidentiality and integrity protection for other keys.
Keying material	A cryptographic key and other parameters (e.g., IVs or domain parameters) used with a cryptographic algorithm.
	When keying material is derived as specified in SP 800-56C[4] and SP 800-108:[5] Data represented as a bit string such that any non-overlapping segments of the string with the required lengths

---

[4] SP 800-56C, *Recommendation for Key Derivation through Extraction-then-Expansion.*
[5] SP 800-108, *Recommendation for Key Derivation Using Pseudorandom Functions.*

can be used as secret keys, secret initialization vectors, and other secret parameters.

Keying relationship, cryptographic	The state existing between two entities such that they share at least one cryptographic key.
Message Authentication Code (MAC)	A cryptographic checksum on data that uses an **approved** security function and a symmetric key to detect both accidental and intentional modifications of data.
Message digest	See *hash value*.
Metadata	The information associated with a key that describes its specific characteristics, constraints, acceptable uses, ownership, etc.; sometimes called the key's attributes.
Mode of operation	An algorithm that uses a block cipher algorithm as a cryptographic primitive to provide a cryptographic service, such as confidentiality or authentication.
NIST standard	Federal Information Processing Standard (FIPS) or Special Publication (SP).
Non-repudiation	A service using a digital signature that is used to support a determination of whether a message was actually signed by a given entity.
Owner of a certificate	The entity that is responsible for managing the certificate, including requesting, replacing, and revoking the certificate if and when required. The certificate owner is not necessarily the subject entity associated with the public key in the certificate (i.e., the key pair owner).
Owner of a key or key pair	One or more entities that are authorized to use a symmetric key or the private key of a key pair.
Plaintext	Data that has not been encrypted; intelligible data that has meaning and can be understood without the application of decryption.
Pre-shared key	A secret key that has previously been established between the parties who are authorized to use it by means of some secure method (e.g., using a secure manual-distribution process or automated key-establishment scheme).
Primitive	See *cryptographic primitive*.
Private key	A cryptographic key used with a public key cryptographic algorithm that is uniquely associated with an entity and is not

made public. In an asymmetric (public) key cryptosystem, the private key is associated with a public key. Depending on the algorithm, the private key may be used to:

1. Compute the corresponding public key,

2. Compute a digital signature that may be verified by the corresponding public key,

3. Decrypt data that was encrypted by the corresponding public key, or

4. Compute a shared secret during a key-agreement process.

Protocol	A set of rules used by two or more communicating entities that describe the message order and data structures for information exchanged between the entities.
Public key	A cryptographic key used with a public-key (asymmetric-key) algorithm that is uniquely associated with an entity and that may be made public. In an asymmetric (public) key cryptosystem, the public key is associated with a private key. The public key may be known by anyone and, depending on the algorithm, may be used to

1. Verify a digital signature that is signed by the corresponding private key,

2. Encrypt data that can be decrypted by the corresponding private key, or

3. Compute a shared secret during a key-agreement process.

Public key (asymmetric-key) cryptographic algorithm	A cryptographic algorithm that uses two related keys: a public key and a private key. The two keys have the property that determining the private key from the public key is computationally infeasible.
Public Key Infrastructure (PKI)	A framework that is established to issue, maintain, and revoke public key certificates.
Random bit generator (RBG)	A device or algorithm that outputs a sequence of bits that appears to be statistically independent and unbiased.
Relying party	An entity that relies on the certificate and the CA that issued the certificate to verify the identity of the certificate owner and the validity of the public key, associated algorithms, and any relevant parameters in the certificate, as well as the owner's possession of the corresponding private key.

RSA

A public-key algorithm that is used for key establishment and the generation and verification of digital signatures.

Scheme

A set of unambiguously specified transformations that provide a (cryptographic) service (e.g., key establishment) when properly implemented and maintained. A scheme is a higher-level construct than a primitive and a lower-level construct than a protocol.

Secret key

A single cryptographic key that is used with a symmetric (secret key) cryptographic algorithm and is not made public (i.e., the key is kept secret). A secret key is also called a symmetric key.

The use of the term "secret" in this context does not imply a classification level, but rather implies the need to protect the key from disclosure.

Compare with a private key, which is used with a public-key (asymmetric-key) algorithm.

Secret-key (symmetric) cryptographic algorithm

See *symmetric (secret key) algorithm*.

Sensitive (information)

Sensitive but unclassified information.

Security function

Cryptographic algorithms, together with modes of operation (if appropriate); for example, block cipher algorithms, digital signature algorithms, asymmetric key-establishment algorithms, message authentication codes, hash functions, or random bit generators. See FIPS 140.[6]

Security strength

A number associated with the amount of work (i.e., the number of operations) that is required to break a cryptographic algorithm or system.

Server

A computer or device on a network that manages network resources. Examples include file servers (to store files), print servers (to manage one or more printers), network servers (to manage network traffic), and database servers (to process database queries).

---

[6] FIPS 140, *Security Requirements for Cryptographic Modules*.

Shall	This term is used to indicate a requirement that needs to be fulfilled to claim conformance to this Recommendation. Note that **shall** may be coupled with **not** to become **shall not**.
Shared secret	A secret value that is computed during a (pair-wise) key-agreement transaction and is used as input to derive a key using a key-derivation method.
Should	When shown in a **bold** font, this term is used to indicate an important recommendation. Ignoring the recommendation could result in undesirable results. Note that **should** may be coupled with **not** to become **should not**.
Signature generation	The use of a digital signature algorithm and a private key to generate a digital signature on data.
Signature verification	The use of a digital signature and a public key to verify a digital signature on data.
Source authentication	The process of providing assurance about the source of information; sometimes called data-origin authentication. Compare with Identity authentication.
Static key pair	A long-term key pair for which the public key is often provided in a public-key certificate.
Symmetric key	A single cryptographic key that is used with a symmetric (secret key) algorithm, is uniquely associated with one or more entities, and is not made public (i.e., the key is kept secret); a symmetric key is often called a secret key.
Symmetric-key (secret-key) algorithm	A cryptographic algorithm that uses the same secret key for an operation and its complement (e.g., encryption and decryption). The key is kept secret and is called either a secret key or symmetric key.

1.6   Acronyms

AES	Advanced Encryption Standard; specified in FIPS 197[7]
ANS	American National Standard
ANSI	American National Standard Institute
ASC	Accredited Standards Committee
CA	Certification Authority
CBC	Cipher Block Chaining mode; specified in SP 800-38A[8]
CFB	Cipher Feedback mode; specified in SP 800-38A

---

[7] FIPS 197, *Advanced Encryption Standard (AES)*.

[8] SP 800-38A, *Recommendation for Block Cipher Modes of Operation: Methods and Techniques*.

CKMS	Cryptographic Key Management System
CP	Certificate Policy
CPS	Certification Practice Statement
CRL	Certificate Revocation List
CTR	Counter Mode; specified in SP 800-38A
DES	Data Encryption Standard; originally specified in FIPS 46; now provided in SP 800-67[9]
DH	Diffie–Hellman algorithm
DNSSEC	Domain Name System Security Extensions
DRBG	Deterministic Random Bit Generator; specified in SP 800-90A[10]
DSA	Digital Signature Algorithm; specified in FIPS 186[11]
ECB	Electronic Codebook mode; specified in SP 800-38A
ECDSA	Elliptic Curve Digital Signature Algorithm
EMC	Electromagnetic Compatibility
FCKMS	Federal Cryptographic Key Management System
FIPS	Federal Information Processing Standard
FISMA	Federal Information Security Management Act
GCM	Galois Counter Mode; specified in SP 800-38D[12]
HMAC	Keyed-Hash Message Authentication Code; specified in FIPS 198[13]
IEC	International Electrotechnical Commission
IEEE	Institute of Electrical and Electronics Engineers
IETF	Internet Engineering Task Force
EMI	Electromagnetic Interference
INCITS	International Committee for Information Technology Standards
IPSEC	Internet Protocol Security
ISO	International Organization for Standardization
IT	Information Technology
KMAC	KECCAK Message Authentication Code; specified in SP 800-185[14]
MAC	Message Authentication Code
MQV	Menezes–Qu–Vanstone algorithm; specified in SP 800-56A[15]
NRBG	Non-deterministic Random Bit Generator
NIST	National Institute of Standards and Technology
OFB	Output Feedback mode; specified in SP 800-38A
OMB	Office of Management and Budget
OTAR	Over-the-Air-Rekeying

---

[9] SP 800-67, *Recommendation for the Triple Data Encryption Algorithm (TDEA) Block Cipher.*

[10] SP 800-90A, *Recommendation for Random Number Generation Using Deterministic Random Bit Generators.*

[11] FIPS 186, *Digital Signature Standard (DSS).*

[12] SP 800-38D, *Recommendation for Block Cipher Modes of Operation: Galois/Counter Mode (GCM) and GMAC.*

[13] FIPS 198, *Keyed-Hash Message Authentication Code (HMAC).*

[14] SP 800-185, *SHA-3 Derived Functions: cSHAKE, KMAC, TupleHash and ParallelHash.*

[15] SP 800-56A, *Recommendation for Pair-Wise Key-Establishment Schemes Using Discrete Logarithm Cryptography.*

PKI	Public Key Infrastructure
RA	Registration Authority
RBG	Random Bit Generator
RFC	Request for Comment
RSA	A public key algorithm attributed to Rivest, Shamir, and Adleman
ROTs	Roots of Trust
SHA	Secure Hash Algorithm
SP	Special Publication
SSH	Secure Shell protocol
TCG	Trusted Computing Group
TDEA	Triple Data Encryption Algorithm; specified in SP 800-67
TLS	Transport Layer Security
TPM	Trusted Platform Module

1.7 Document Organization

This document is organized into the following sections:

- Section 1 provides an introduction to the SP 800-175 series of publications and to this document in particular, and provides a glossary of terms and a list of acronyms.

- Section 2 discusses the importance of standards, as well as the national and international standards bodies concerned with cryptography.

- Section 3 introduces the **approved** algorithms used for encryption, digital signatures, and key-establishment and provides discussions on security strengths and algorithm lifetime.

- Section 4 discusses the services that cryptography can provide, including data confidentiality, data integrity authentication, identity authentication, source authentication, and support for non-repudiation.

- Section 5 discusses the key management required for the use of cryptography, providing general guidance and discussions on key-management systems, key-establishment mechanisms, and random bit generation.

- Section 6 discusses additional issues associated with the use of cryptography.

- The References section lists applicable Federal Information Processing Standards, NIST Recommendations, and guidelines.

- Appendix A provides a list of revisions since the original publication of this document.

2   Standards and Guidelines

2.1   Benefits of Standards

Standards define common practices, methods, measures, and metrics. Standards provide solutions that have been evaluated by experts in relevant areas, reviewed by the public, and subsequently accepted by a wide community of users. By using standards, organizations can reduce costs and protect their investments in technology.

Standards provide the following benefits:

- **Interoperability.** Products developed to a specific standard may be used to provide interoperability with other products that conform to the same standard. For example, by using the same cryptographic encryption algorithm, data that was encrypted using vendor A's product may be decrypted using vendor B's product. The use of a common standards-based cryptographic algorithm is necessary but may not be sufficient to ensure product interoperability. Other common standards, such as communications protocol standards, may also be necessary.

  By ensuring interoperability among the products of different vendors, standards permit an organization to select from various available products to find the most cost-effective solution.

- **Security.** Standards may be used to establish a common level of security. For example, most agency managers are not cryptographic security experts, and by using an **approved** cryptographic algorithm and key length, a manager knows that the algorithm has been found to be adequate for the protection of sensitive government data and has been subjected to a significant period of public analysis and comment.

- **Quality.** Standards may be used to assure the quality of a product. Standards may

  - o Specify how a feature is to be implemented,

  - o Require self-tests to ensure that the product is still functioning correctly, and

  - o Require specific documentation to assure proper implementation and product-change management.

  Many NIST standards have associated conformance tests and specify the conformance requirements. The conformance tests may be administered by NIST-accredited laboratories and provide validation that the NIST standard was correctly implemented.

- **Common Form of Reference.** A NIST standard may become a common form of reference to be used in testing or evaluating a vendor's product. For example, FIPS 140 contains security and integrity requirements for any cryptographic module implementing cryptographic operations.

- **Cost Savings.** Implementations that comply with commonly accepted specifications provided by standards can save money. Without standards, users may be required to become experts in every information technology (IT) product that is being considered for procurement. Also, without standards, products may not interoperate with different products purchased by other users. This could result in a significant waste of money or in the delay of implementing an IT solution.

2.2   Federal Information Processing Standards and Special Publications

2.2.1   The Use of FIPS and SPs

The use of a Federal Information Processing Standard (FIPS) is *mandatory* for the Federal Government whenever the type of functionality specified in that standard is required by a federal agency for the protection of sensitive information.[16] For example, FIPS 197 contains a specific set of technical security requirements for the AES algorithm. Whenever AES is used by an agency, its implementation and use must conform to FIPS 197. A FIPS is **approved** by the Secretary of Commerce.

A NIST Special Publication (SP) is similar to a FIPS but is not mandatory unless a particular government agency (e.g., OMB) makes it so. An SP does not need the approval of the Secretary of Commerce.

Although the requirements for the use of a FIPS and an SP are different, both types of publications have been subjected to the same review process by the federal agencies and the public. The approval process for a FIPS is more formal than that of an SP and subsequently takes longer for the initial approval and the approval of any subsequent revisions. See NIST 7977[17] for the complete development process of NIST standards and guidelines.

When a federal agency requires the use of cryptography (e.g., for encryption), an **approved** algorithm must be used; approval is indicated by inclusion in a FIPS or SP. For example, AES (as specified in FIPS 197) is an **approved** algorithm. Whenever encryption is used by a federal agency for the protection of sensitive information, an **approved** encryption algorithm must be implemented and used as specified. In addition to using **approved** algorithms, federal agencies are required to use only implementations of these algorithms that have been validated and are included in validated cryptographic modules (see Section 5.4.5 for further discussion).

When developing a specification or the criteria for the selection of a cryptographic mechanism or service, cryptographic algorithms specified in FIPS and SPs must be used, when available. Some guidelines may be used to specify the functions that the algorithm will perform (e.g., FIPS 199[18] or SP 800-53).[19] Other NIST standards specify the operation and use of specific types of algorithms (e.g., AES, ECDSA) and the level of independent testing required for classes of security environments (e.g., FIPS 140).

---

[16] FISMA 2002 as reformed by FISMA 2014 and OMB Circular A-130, Appendix III. Also, see Public Law 107-347 as extended by Public law 113-283.

[17] NIST 7977, *NIST Cryptographic Standards and Guidelines Development Process.*

[18] FIPS 199, *Standards for Security Categorization of Federal Information and Information Systems.*

[19] SP 800-53, *Security and Privacy Controls for Federal Information Systems and Organizations.*

Appendix A contains a list of FIPS and SPs that apply to the implementation of cryptography in the Federal Government. Note that when a FIPS is revised, its number is commonly followed by a revision number that indicates the number of times that it has been revised (e.g., "FIPS 186-4" is used to indicate the fourth revision of FIPS 186); when an SP is revised, an indication of its revision status follows its number (i.e., Rev. 1). This practice is not used in the main body of this document; the reader must refer to the latest version of the FIPS or SP that has been officially **approved** (see https://csrc.nist.gov/publications/; note that this site also contains clearly marked draft publications).

2.2.2 NIST Interagency/Internal Reports

Another publication developed by NIST is a NIST Interagency/Internal Report (NISTIR), which is a public document developed within NIST (Internal) or in collaboration with other agencies (Interagency). A NISTIR is often used to present research that supports subsequent FIPS and SPs. However, discussion of this type of publication is out-of-scope for this document (i.e, SP 800-175B).

2.2.3 FIPS Waivers

In the past, a waiver was sometimes issued by an agency to indicate that the use of a FIPS was not required by that agency. However, the Federal Information Security Management Act (FISMA) of 2002 (P.L. 107-347) eliminated previously authorized provisions for waivers from FIPS. The prohibition of waivers (except by the President) has been retained in subsequent cybersecurity legislation. (See SP 800-175A for a discussion of legislative mandates and executive direction.).

2.3 Other Standards Organizations

NIST develops standards and guidelines that are used by vendors who are developing security products, components, and modules. These products may be acquired and used by Federal Government agencies. In addition, there are other groups that develop and promulgate standards. These organizations are briefly described below.

2.3.1 American National Standards Institute (ANSI)[20]

The American National Standards Institute (ANSI) is the administrator and coordinator of the United States' private-sector voluntary standardization system. ANSI does not develop American National Standards itself; rather, it facilitates the development of standards by establishing consensus among qualified groups.

Several ANSI committees have developed standards that use cryptography, but the primary committee that has developed standards for the cryptographic algorithms themselves is Accredited Standards Committee (ASC) X9, which is a financial-industry committee.[21] Many of the standards developed within ASC X9 have been adopted within NIST standards (e.g., the Elliptic Curve Digital Signature Algorithm specified in American National

---

[20] Further information is available at the ANSI web site: www.ansi.org.

[21] Further information is available at the ANSI X9 web site: x9.org.

Standard X9.62[22] has been adopted in FIPS 186). Likewise, ASC X9 has approved the use of NIST standards via a registry of approved standards from non-ASC X9 sources (e.g., AES, as specified in FIPS 197).

A number of ASC X9 standards have also been incorporated into the standards of other standards bodies, such as the International Organization for Standardization (ISO) (see Section 2.3.4) via a Technical Advisory Group (TAG) called the International Committee on Information Technology Standards (INCITS). INCITS has been responsible for assuring that U.S. standards (e.g., both those developed by NIST and those developed within ASC X9) are incorporated within ISO standards.

2.3.2 Institute of Electrical and Electronics Engineers (IEEE) Standards Association[23]

IEEE is an international, professional association that is dedicated to advancing technological innovation and excellence. The technical objectives of the IEEE focus on advancing the theory and practice of electrical, electronics and computer engineering, and computer science. IEEE develops and disseminates voluntary, consensus-based industry standards involving leading-edge electro-technology. IEEE supports international standardization and encourages the development of globally acceptable standards.

The Institute of Electrical and Electronics Engineers Standards Association (IEEE-SA) is an organization within IEEE that develops global standards. It has more than one thousand active standards, some of which are related to cryptography.

IEEE 1363[24] is the only IEEE standard that focuses on cryptography and includes a series of standards on public-key cryptography. IEEE 1363 was developed at the same time as many of the ANSI public-key cryptographic standards that were developed in ASC X9 (see Section 2.3.1).

- The first part of the IEEE 1363 standard was published in 2000 and revised in 2004 as IEEE 1363a.[25] It includes the basic public-key cryptography schemes, such as RSA encryption, digital signatures, the Digital Signature Algorithm (DSA), and key establishment using Diffie–Hellman (DH) and Menezes–Qu–Vanstone (MQV) over finite fields and elliptic curves.

- IEEE 1363.1,[26] which was published in 2008, specifies NTRU encryption and signature schemes.

- IEEE 1363.2[27] was also published in 2008. It specifies password-authenticated key agreement and password-authenticated key retrieval schemes.

The schemes specified in IEEE 1363.1 and 1363.2 are not included in the NIST standards.

---

[22] ANS X9.62, *Public Key Cryptography for the Financial Services Industry: The Elliptic Curve Digital Signature Algorithm (ECDSA)*.

[23] Further information is available at the IEEE-SA web site: standards.ieee.org.

[24] IEEE 1363, Standard Specifications for Public-Key Cryptography.

[25] IEEE 1363a, *Standard Specifications for Public Key Cryptography - Amendment 1: Additional Techniques*.

[26] IEEE 1363.1, *Public-Key Cryptographic Techniques Based on Hard Problems over Lattices*.

[27] IEEE 1363.2, *Password-Based Public-Key Cryptography*.

Cryptographic schemes are used in IEEE standards for different applications. One of the more notable is the IEEE 802 LAN/MAN[28] group of standards, which are widely used computer networking standards for both wired (Ethernet) and wireless (IEEE 802.11)[29] networks. Cryptographic algorithms are used to protect wireless communications. The CCM mode for authentication and confidentiality specified in SP 800-38C[30] was adopted from IEEE 802.11. Other AES modes of operation (e.g., GCM, which is specified in SP 800-38D) are also used in IEEE 802 standards. IEEE 802 standards also use the SHA-1 and SHA-2 family of hash functions specified in FIPS 180[31] and used in HMAC, as specified in FIPS 198.

XTS, a block cipher mode of operation specified in SP 800-38E,[32] was adopted from IEEE 1619.[33]

2.3.3 Internet Engineering Task Force (IETF)[34]

The Internet Engineering Task Force (IETF) is an international community of network designers, operators, vendors, researchers, and technologists who work on the Internet architecture and its techniques and protocols. An IETF official technical specification or recommendation is called a Request for Comments (RFC).

The technical work of the IETF is done in its working groups, which are organized by topic into several areas, such as routing, transport, and security. In the security area, different working groups are formed when needed to develop different security mechanisms for security protocols or applications. For example:

1. The PKIX (Public-Key Infrastructure X.509) Working Group (PKIX-WG) developed technical specifications and recommendations to support a Public Key Infrastructure based on the X.509[35] protocol, which is used to build a trust and authentication services infrastructure.

2. The IPSEC (Internet Protocol Security) working group developed a protocol and other technical recommendations for secure routing between network devices.

3. The TLS (Transport Layer Security) working group has been specifying a communication protocol and technical recommendations to provide security services for communication between a server and a client.

NIST-approved cryptographic algorithms – such as block cipher modes of operation, hash functions, key-establishment schemes, and digital signatures – are used in various IETF

---

[28] LAN/MAN: Local Area Network (LAN) and Metropolitan Area Network (MAN)

[29] IEEE 802.11, *Wireless Local Area Networks*.

[30] SP 800-38C, *Recommendation for Block Cipher Modes of Operation: the CCM Mode for Authentication and Confidentiality.*

[31] FIPS 180, *Secure Hash Standard (SHS).*

[32] SP 800-38E, *Recommendation for Block Cipher Modes of Operation: the XTS-AES Mode for Confidentiality on Storage Devices.*

[33] IEEE 1619, *Standard for Cryptographic Protection of Data on Block-Oriented Storage Devices.*

[34] Further information is available at the IETF web site, https://www.ietf.org/.

[35] X.509, *Information technology - Open Systems Interconnection -The Directory: Public-key and attribute certificate frameworks.*

protocols. For example, RFC 5288[36] specifies the AES Galois Counter Mode (GCM) Cipher Suites based on SP 800-38D for TLS.

2.3.4 International Organization for Standardization (ISO)[37]

ISO is a non-governmental, worldwide federation of national standards bodies. Its mission is to develop international standards that help make industry more efficient and effective. ISO standards cover almost all aspects of technology and business, from food safety to computers, and from agriculture to healthcare. Experts from all over the world develop the standards that are required by the nation or liaison organization they represent using a consensus process.

ISO/IEC JTC 1 is a joint technical committee of the International Organization for Standardization (ISO) and the International Electrotechnical Commission (IEC). ISO/IEC JTC 1 SC 27 is the subcommittee for IT security. Working group 2 (WG2) is the group developing standards for cryptography and security mechanisms. It usually has more than 20 active projects to develop either a revision of an existing standard or a new standard. Each standard consists of multiple parts, and each part includes multiple algorithms and/or mechanisms.

The cryptographic algorithms and schemes in FIPS and SPs are usually included in ISO/IEC standards, along with many other algorithms submitted by other countries. The following is a list of ISO/IEC standards that include cryptographic algorithms and schemes specified in NIST standards.

1. ISO/IEC 9797-1, *Information technology − Security techniques − Message Authentication Codes (MACs) – Part 1: Mechanisms using a block cipher.*

2. ISO/IEC 9797-2, *Information technology − Security techniques − Message Authentication Codes (MACs) – Part 2: Mechanisms using a dedicated hash-function.*

3. ISO/IEC 10116, *Information technology − Security techniques − Modes of operation for an n-bit block cipher.*

4. ISO/IEC 10118-3, *Information technology − Security techniques − Hash-functions – Part 3: Dedicated hash-functions.*

5. ISO/IEC 11770-3, *Information technology − Security techniques − Key management – Part 3: Mechanisms using asymmetric techniques.*

6. ISO/IEC 11770-6, *Information technology − Security techniques − Key management – Part 6: Key derivation.*

7. ISO/IEC 14888-2, *Information technology − Security techniques − Digital signatures with appendix – Part 2: Integer factorization based mechanisms.*

8. ISO/IEC CD 14888-3, *Information technology − Security techniques − Digital signatures with appendix – Part 3: Discrete logarithm based mechanisms.*

---

[36] RFC 5288, *AES Galois Counter Mode (GCM) Cipher Suites for TLS.*

[37] Further information is available at the ISO web site, https://www.iso.org/.

9. ISO/IEC 18033-3, *Information technology − Security techniques − Encryption algorithms − Part 3: Block ciphers.*

10. ISO/IEC 19772, *Information technology − Security techniques − Authenticated encryption.*

2.3.5 Trusted Computing Group (TCG)

The Trusted Computing Group (TCG) develops and promotes a set of industry standards that build upon roots of trust. Roots of Trust (RoTs) are hardware, firmware, and software components that are inherently trusted to perform specific, vital security functions. Because misbehavior by RoTs may not be detected, they must be secure by design. To ensure that they are reliable and resistant to tampering, RoTs are often implemented in or protected by hardware.

Industry standards developed by the TCG define the capabilities of a set of fundamental roots of trust and describe how to use those roots of trust in a variety of architectures and use cases. Many of the use cases supported by TCG technologies and specifications focus on one or more of the following areas: 1) device identity, 2) cryptographic key or credential storage, and 3) attestation of the system state.

Technologies supporting TCG-developed standards are deployed as enterprise-class clients and servers, storage devices, embedded systems, and virtualized devices. Families of relevant TCG standards and specifications include:

- Trusted Platform Modules (TPMs): A TPM is a cryptographic module that can, among other capabilities, establish device identity in a platform, provide secure storage for keys and credentials, and support the measurement and reporting of the system state. The TPM 2.0 Library Specification provides the general architecture and command set for TPMs, with platform-specific specifications detailing how a TPM can be implemented in particular classes of systems. ISO/IEC JTC 1 has approved the TPM Library Specification as ISO/IEC 11889:2015 Parts 1−4.[38]

- Trusted Network Connect (TNC): The TCG's TNC Working Group defines specifications that allow network administrators to enforce policies regarding endpoint integrity on devices connected to a network. These specifications were the basis for much of the work in the IETF's Network Endpoint Assessment (NEA) working group and are highly complementary to the ongoing work in the IETF Security Automation and Continuous Monitoring (SACM) working group.

- Storage: The TCG's Storage Working Group defines specifications that enable standards-based mechanisms to protect data on storage devices and manage these devices and capabilities. The TCG's storage specifications break out from a common core specification into two Security Subsystem Classes (SSCs): the Opal SSC, which is intended for client devices (e.g., tablets, notebooks and desktops), and the Enterprise SSC, which is intended for high-performance storage systems (e.g., servers).

---

[38] ISO/IEC 11889:2015 Parts 1-4, *Trusted Platform Module; Part 1: Architecture, Part 2: Structures, Part 3: Commands, and Part 4: Supporting Routines.*

3   Cryptographic Algorithms

This document describes three types of cryptographic algorithms: cryptographic hash functions, symmetric-key algorithms, and asymmetric-key algorithms, which are discussed in Sections 3.1, 3.2, and 3.3, respectively. Other topics to be introduced in this section include the concept of algorithm security strength and algorithm lifetime (see Sections 3.4 and 3.5, respectively).

3.1   Cryptographic Hash Functions

A hash function (also called a hash algorithm) is a cryptographic primitive algorithm that produces a condensed representation of its input (e.g., a message). A hash function takes an input of arbitrary length and outputs a value with a predetermined length. Common names for the output of a hash function include *hash value* and *message digest.*

A cryptographic hash function is a one-way function that is extremely difficult to invert. That is, it is not practical to reverse the process from the hash value back to the input.

Figure 1 depicts the process of generating and verifying a hash value.

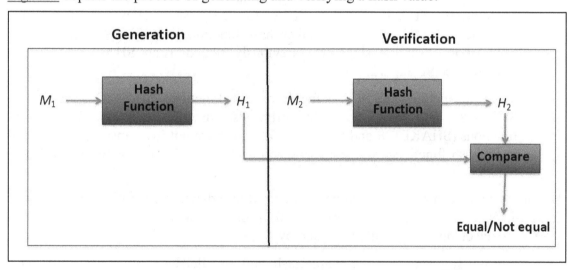

Figure 1: Hash Function Generation and Verification

A hash function is used as follows:

- Hash Generation:

    1. A hash value (H_1) is generated on data (M_1) using the hash function.

    2. M_1 and H_1 are then saved or transmitted.

- Hash Verification:

    1. A hash value (H_2) is generated on the received or retrieved data (M_2) using the same hash function that generated H_1.

    2. H_1 and H_2 are compared. If $H_1 = H_2$, then it can be assumed that M_1 has not changed during storage or transmission.

The above description is for the simplest use of a hash function. Hash functions are usually used in higher-level algorithms, including

- Keyed-hash message authentication code algorithms (Sections 3.2.2 and 4.2.2.2),

- Digital signature algorithms (Section 4.2.3),

- Key derivation functions (e.g., for key establishment) (Section 5.3.2), and

- Random bit generators (Section 4.4).

Approved hash functions for Federal Government use are specified in FIPS 180, FIPS 202,[39] and SP 800-185.

- FIPS 180 specifies the SHA-1 hash function and the SHA-2 family of hash functions: SHA-224, SHA-256, SHA-384, SHA-512, SHA-512/224, and SHA-512/256. Additional guidance for the use of these hash functions is provided in SP 800-106[40] and SP 800-107.[41]

  Note that attacks on SHA-1 have indicated that SHA-1 provides less security than originally thought when generating digital signatures (see Section 4.2.3); consequently, SHA-1 is now disallowed for that purpose. However, SHA-1 may continue to be used for most other hash-function applications, including the verification of digital signatures previously signed using SHA-1 as the hash function (see SP 800-131A).[42]

- FIPS 202 specifies the SHA-3 family of hash functions: SHA3-224, SHA3-256, SHA3-384, and SHA3-512. This FIPS also specifies two extendable-output functions (SHAKE128 and SHAKE256), which are not in themselves considered to be hash functions. SP 800-185 specifies **approved** uses for SHAKE128 and SHAKE256.

The numbers in each hash function name are used to indicate the length of the output of that hash function (e.g., SHA-1 produces 160 bit outputs, while SHA-XXX and SHA3-XXX produce outputs of a length indicated by XXX.

- SP 800-185 specifies the TupleHash and ParallelHash functions. Both hash functions can produce variable-length output. TupleHash is designed to hash tuples of input. ParallelHash is a variable-length hash function that can hash contiguous, non-overlapping blocks of very long messages in parallel.

3.2   Symmetric-Key Algorithms

Symmetric-key algorithms (sometimes called secret-key algorithms) use a single key to both apply cryptographic protection and to remove or check the protection (i.e., the same key is used for a cryptographic operation and its inverse). For example, the key used to

---

[39] FIPS 202, *SHA-3 Standard: Permutation-Based Hash and Extendable Output Functions.*

[40] SP 800-106, *Randomized Hashing for Digital Signatures.*

[41] SP 800-107, *Recommendations for Applications Using Approved Hash Algorithms.*

[42] SP 800-131A, *Transitions: Recommendation for Transitioning the Use of Cryptographic Algorithms and Key Lengths.*

encrypt data (i.e., apply protection) is also used to decrypt the encrypted data (i.e., remove the protection). In the case of encryption, the original data is called the plaintext, while the encrypted form of the data is called the ciphertext. The key must be kept secret if the data is to remain protected.

Several classes of symmetric-key algorithms have been approved: those based on block cipher algorithms (e.g., AES) and those based on the use of hash functions (e.g., a keyed-hash message authentication code based on SHA-1).

Symmetric-key algorithms are used for

- Encryption to provide data confidentiality (see Section 4.1),

- Authentication to provide assurance of data integrity and the source of the data (see Section 4.2),

- Key derivation (see Section 5.3.2),

- Key wrapping (see Section 5.3.5), and

- Random bit generation (see Section 4.4).

When using a symmetric-key algorithm, a unique key needs to be generated for each cryptographic relationship[43] and for each purpose (e.g., encryption, data integrity authentication, and key wrapping). Technically, the same key can be used for multiple purposes when the same algorithm is used, but this is usually ill-advised, as the use of the same key for two different cryptographic processes (e.g., HMAC and key derivation using the same hash function) may weaken the security provided by one or both of the processes. However, exceptions to this rule have been approved (see Section 4.3).

As an example of the number of keys required for the use of symmetric-key algorithms, suppose that there are four entities (A, B, C, and D) that need to communicate using encryption, with each pair of entities using a different encryption key. There are six possible pair-wise relationships (A-B, A-C, A-D, B-C, B-D, and C-D), so at least six keys are required.[44] If, instead, there are 1,000 entities that wish to communicate with each other, there are 499,500 possible pair-wise relationships, and at least one unique key would be required for each relationship. If more than one algorithm, key length, or purpose is to be supported (e.g., both encryption and key wrapping), then additional keys will be needed. Each entity must keep all its symmetric keys secret and protect their integrity. The need for a large number of keying relationships is a significant problem; methods for mitigating this problem are discussed in Section 5.

Several symmetric-key algorithms have been **approved** by NIST for the protection of sensitive data. However, some of these algorithms are no longer approved for applying cryptographic protection (e.g., encryption) but may continue to be used for processing already-protected information (e.g., decryption), provided that the risk of doing so is

---

[43] A cryptographic relationship exists when two or more parties can communicate using the same key and algorithm. A relationship may be one-to-one or one-to-many (e.g., broadcast).

[44] Although only six cryptographic relationships are used in the example, different keys may be required by some protocols for each communication direction (i.e., a different key may be required for communications sent from A to B than is used for communications sent from B to A).

acceptable (e.g., there is reason to believe that a key was not compromised). See SP 800-57, Part 1 and SP 800-131A for more information about the acceptability of using the different cryptographic algorithms.

3.2.1 Block Cipher Algorithms

A block cipher algorithm is used with a single key in an **approved** mode of operation to both apply cryptographic protection (e.g., encrypt) and to subsequently process the protected information (e.g., decrypt). Several block cipher algorithms have been approved by NIST as cryptographic primitives, some of which are no longer approved for applying cryptographic protection. However, they may still be needed for processing information that was previously protected (e.g., they may be needed for decrypting previously encrypted information).

The block cipher algorithms are discussed in Sections 3.2.1.1 through 3.2.1.4. **Approved** modes of operation are discussed in Section 3.2.1.5.

3.2.1.1 Data Encryption Standard (DES)

The Data Encryption Standard (DES) was approved in July 1977, and was the first NIST-**approved** cryptographic algorithm. It was reaffirmed several times, but due to advances in computer power and speeds, the strength of the DES algorithm is no longer sufficient to adequately protect Federal Government information. Therefore, DES was withdrawn as an **approved** algorithm in 2005 (i.e., the use of DES is no longer approved for encryption or otherwise applying cryptographic protection). However, the DES "cryptographic engine" continues to be used as a component function of TDEA (see the next section).

3.2.1.2 Triple Data Encryption Algorithm (TDEA)

The Triple Data Encryption Algorithm (TDEA), also known as Triple DES, uses the DES cryptographic engine to transform data in three operations (see SP 800-67). TDEA encrypts data in blocks of 64 bits using three keys that define a key bundle. Two variations of TDEA have been defined: two-key TDEA (2TDEA), in which the first and third keys are identical, and three-key TDEA (3TDEA), in which the three keys are all different (i.e., distinct).

A number of attacks on TDEA have been published that indicate that the security life of TDEA is nearing its conclusion, so NIST announced plans[45] to discontinue approval for the use of TDEA for federal applications. A schedule has been published in SP 800-131A.

The use of 2TDEA is **disallowed** for applying cryptographic protection (e.g., for encrypting plaintext data). However, 2TDEA may continue to be used for processing already-protected information (e.g., for decrypting ciphertext data), although the user must accept some risk that increases over time. For example, if the data was encrypted and transmitted over public networks when the algorithm was still considered secure, the ciphertext may have been captured (by an adversary) at that time and later decrypted by that adversary when the algorithm was no longer considered secure; thus, the confidentiality of the data would no longer be assured.

---

[45] See https://csrc.nist.gov/news/2017/update-to-current-use-and-deprecation-of-tdea.

The use of 3TDEA for applying cryptographic protection (e.g., encrypting) has been **deprecated** in favor of other **approved** block ciphers (i.e., the user must accept some risk when using the algorithm to apply protection). In addition, SP 800-67 includes a restriction on the amount of data that can be protected with a single three-key bundle. Federal applications **shall** only use three distinct keys whenever using TDEA for applying cryptographic protection. After December 31, 2023, 3TDEA will be **disallowed** for applying cryptographic protection but may continue to be used for processing already-protected information, again with the stipulation that the user must accept some security risk.

3.2.1.3 SKIPJACK

SKIPJACK is referenced in FIPS 185[46] and specified in a classified document. SKIPJACK is no longer considered adequate for the protection of federal information and has been withdrawn as a FIPS. The use of SKIPJACK for applying cryptographic protection (e.g., encryption) is **disallowed**, although it is permissible to use the algorithm for decrypting information.

3.2.1.4 Advanced Encryption Standard (AES)

The Advanced Encryption Standard (AES) was developed as a replacement for DES and TDEA and is the preferred block cipher algorithm for new products. AES is specified in FIPS 197. AES operates on 128-bit blocks of data, using 128, 192, or 256-bit keys. The nomenclature for AES for the different key sizes is AES-x, where x is the key size (i.e., AES-128, AES-192, and AES-256). The use of AES is acceptable (i.e., considered secure) for all AES applications, although the key size may be a factor when using AES (see Section 3.4).

3.2.1.5 Modes of Operation

With a symmetric-key block cipher algorithm, the same input block will always produce the same output block when the same key is used. If the multiple blocks in a typical message are encrypted separately, an adversary can easily substitute individual blocks, possibly without detection. Furthermore, certain kinds of data patterns in the plaintext, such as repeated blocks, would be apparent in the ciphertext. To counteract these properties, modes of operation have been specified for using a block cipher algorithm.

These modes combine the cryptographic primitive algorithm with a symmetric key and variable starting values (commonly known as initialization vectors) to provide some cryptographic service (e.g., the encryption of a message or the generation of a message authentication code). **Approved** modes for block cipher algorithms have been specified in the SP 800-38 series of publications and include modes for:

- Encryption, as specified in SP 800-38A, SP 800-38E, and SP 800-38G[47] (see Section 4.1),

---

[46] FIPS 185, *Escrowed Encryption Standard.*

[47] SP 800-38G, *Recommendation for Block Cipher Modes of Operation: Methods for Format-Preserving Encryption.*

- Authentication, as specified in SP 800-38B[48] (see Section 4.2.2.1),

- Authenticated encryption, as specified in SP 800-38C and SP 800-38D (see Section 4.3), and

- Key wrapping, as specified in SP 800-38F (see Section 5.3.5).

3.2.2 Hash-based Symmetric-key Algorithms

A symmetric-key algorithm based on the use of a hash function has been specified in FIPS 198 for generating a message authentication code (MAC). This algorithm, known as HMAC, has been **approved** for use with any **approved** hash function specified in FIPS 180 or FIPS 202. Guidance on the use of the hash functions specified in FIPS 180 for HMAC is provided in SP 800-107.

SP 800-185 specifies an additional MAC algorithm, known as KMAC, which is based on the extendable output function specified in FIPS 202. KMAC has two variants: KMAC128 and KMAC256.

3.3 Asymmetric-Key Algorithms

Asymmetric-key algorithms (often called public-key algorithms) use a pair of keys (i.e., a key pair): a public key and a private key that are mathematically related to each other. The public key may be made public without reducing the security of the process, but the private key must remain secret if the cryptographic protection is to remain effective. Even though there is a relationship between the two keys, the private key cannot efficiently be determined based on knowledge of the public key.

One of the keys of the key pair is used to apply cryptographic protection, and the other key is used to remove or verify that protection. The key to use depends on the algorithm used and the service to be provided. For example, a digital signature is computed using a private key, and the signature is verified using the public key (i.e., the protection is applied using the private key and verified using the corresponding public key). For those asymmetric algorithms also capable of encryption,[49] the encryption is performed using the public key, and the decryption is performed using the private key (i.e., the protection is applied using the public key and removed using the private key).

Asymmetric-key algorithms are used, for example,

1. To provide identity, integrity, and source authentication services in the form of digital signatures (see Sections 3.3.1 and 4.2.3); and

2. To establish cryptographic keying material using key-agreement and key-transport algorithms (see Sections 3.3.2 and 5.3).

These algorithms tend to be much slower than symmetric-key algorithms so are not used to process large amounts of data. However, when used for key establishment (see Section 5), there are methods that combine the use of symmetric and asymmetric algorithms to

---

[48] SP 800-38B, *Recommendation for Block Cipher Modes of Operation: the CMAC Mode for Authentication.*

[49] Not all public-key algorithms are capable of multiple functions (e.g., both encryption and decryption and the generation and verification of digital signatures).

achieve better efficiency than is possible when using only asymmetric algorithms, while reducing the number of keys required when using only symmetric algorithms.

Key pairs for asymmetric-key algorithms **should** be generated for each purpose (e.g., one key pair for generating and verifying digital signatures and a different key pair for key establishment). Technically, it is sometimes possible to use the same key pair for more than one purpose, but this is ill-advised as the use of the same key pair for two different cryptographic purposes (e.g., digital signatures and key establishment) may weaken the security provided by one or both of the processes.

The use of asymmetric-key algorithms requires the establishment of fewer initial keys than the use of symmetric-key algorithms. As an example, suppose that an entity wants to generate digital signatures and participate in a key-establishment process using its own key pair;[50] a key pair needs to be generated for each purpose. If there are six entities that intend to both generate digital signatures and participate in the key-establishment process, then six key pairs are needed for digital signature generation, and another six key pairs are needed for key establishment, for a total of twelve key pairs. For 1,000 entities, 1,000 key pairs of each would be needed for each purpose, for a total of 2,000 key pairs. A unique key pair does not need to be generated for each relationship; recall that for symmetric-key algorithms, a unique key <u>does</u> need to be generated for each relationship (see Section 3.2). If multiple public-key algorithms or key lengths are to be used for either process, then additional key pairs will be required.

The private key is retained and used by the entity who "owns" the key pair; it must be kept secret and its integrity protected. The public key is usually distributed to other entities and requires integrity protection but not confidentiality protection; distribution is often accomplished by using a public-key certificate, as discussed in Section 5.2.3. When a public-key certificate is used, the certificate provides the integrity protection for the public key, so the burden of key protection by each entity is limited to only those private keys owned by the entity.

Some asymmetric-key algorithms use domain parameters, which are additional values necessary for the use of the cryptographic algorithm. These values are mathematically related to each other and to the keys with which they will be used. Domain parameters are usually public and are used by a community of users for a substantial period of time. These domain parameters are either contained within or referenced by a certificate containing a public key.

The secure use of asymmetric-key algorithms is dependent on users obtaining certain assurances:

- Assurance of domain-parameter validity (for those algorithms requiring domain parameters) provides confidence that the domain parameters are mathematically correct,

---

[50] Note that some key-establishment schemes do not require that all parties have key-pairs, so some parties will not need a key pair for key establishment.

- Assurance of public-key validity provides confidence that the public key appears to be a suitable key, and

- Assurance of private-key possession provides confidence that the entity that is supposedly the owner of the private key really has the key.

Important note: When large-scale quantum computers become available, they will threaten the security of the **approved** asymmetric-key algorithms. In particular, the digital signature schemes, key-agreement schemes using Diffie–Hellman and MQV,[51] and the key-agreement and key-transport schemes using RSA may need to be replaced with secure quantum-resistant (or "post-quantum") counterparts. At the time that this revision of SP 800-175B was published, NIST was undergoing a process to select post-quantum cryptographic algorithms for standardization. This process is a multi-year project; when these new standards are available, this document will be updated appropriately. See https://csrc.nist.gov/Topics/Security-and-Privacy/cryptography/post-quantum-cryptography for the status of this effort.

3.3.1 Digital Signature Algorithms

Digital signatures are used to provide identity authentication, integrity authentication, source authentication, and support for non-repudiation. Digital signatures are used in conjunction with hash functions and are computed on data of any length (up to a limit that is determined by the hash function). FIPS 186 specifies algorithms that are **approved** for the computation of digital signatures.[52] It specifies the Digital Signature Algorithm (DSA), and the Elliptic Curve Digital Signature Algorithm (ECDSA) as well as adopting the RSA algorithm as specified in RFC 8017[53] and PKCS 1[54] (version 1.5 and higher) and the Edwards-Curve Digital Signature Algorithm (EdDSA) specified in RFC 8032.[55]

FIPS 186 also specifies several **approved** key sizes for each of these algorithms and includes methods for generating the algorithm's key pairs and many other parameters needed for digital signature generation and verification. However, SP 800-186 (a new publication) contains the recommended elliptic curves to be used with ECDSA and EdDSA.

Digital signature generation **shall** be performed using keys that meet or exceed the key sizes specified in FIPS 186 and using key pairs that are generated in accordance with FIPS 186. Smaller key sizes **shall only** be used to verify signatures that were generated using those smaller keys. See SP 800-131A. (Older systems (legacy systems) used smaller key sizes than those currently approved in FIPS 186.)

---

[51] Both finite field and elliptic curve versions.

[52] Two general types of digital signature methods are discussed in literature: digital signatures with appendix and digital signatures with message recovery. FIPS 186 specifies algorithms for digital signatures with appendix and is the digital signature method that is discussed in this Recommendation.

[53] RFC 8017, *RSA Cryptography Specifications Version 2.2*.

[54] PKCS 1, *RSA Cryptographic Standard 1*.

[55] RFC 8032, *Edwards-Curve Digital Signature Algorithm (EdDSA)*.

3.3.1.1   DSA

The Digital Signature Algorithm (DSA) is specified in FIPS 186 and is approved as of the time of publication of this document. This algorithm is used to generate and verify digital signatures using finite-fields. FIPS 186 defines methods for generating DSA domain parameters and key pairs and specifies the key lengths to be used for secure interoperability and the algorithms to be used for digital-signature generation and verification.

A recent draft of FIPS 186 (i.e., FIPS 186-5) has proposed the removal of DSA from the Standard. If this proposal is adopted, DSA will become **disallowed** for future use. The reader **should** examine the status of FIPS 186-5 before using it.

3.3.1.2   ECDSA

The Elliptic Curve Digital Signature Algorithm (ECDSA) is **approved** and specified in FIPS 186. The basic signature and verification algorithms are the same as those used for DSA, except that the mathematics is based on the use of elliptic curves rather than finite fields. FIPS 186 provides guidance for the use of ECDSA within the Federal Government, and SP 800-186 contains the elliptic curves to be used with ECDSA. An advantage of using ECDSA instead of DSA and RSA is that the key lengths are considerably shorter, requiring less storage space and transmission bandwidth, and the execution of the algorithm is generally faster than DSA and RSA.

FIPS 186 includes specifications for the generation of the ECDSA domain parameters and key pairs, as well as the algorithms for digital signature generation and verification; defines the key lengths to be used for secure interoperability; and provides additional guidance on the use of random bit generators to generate the key pairs.

3.3.1.3   EdDSA

EdDSA is adopted in FIPS 186 and described in RFC 8032, which includes recommended parameters for the Ed25519 and Ed448 curves provided in the RFC. These curves are also included in SP 800-186. While ECDSA (and DSA) signatures require the use of a random (unique) value for the generation of each signature, EdDSA signatures are deterministic: the unique value is computed using the private key and the message to be signed (i.e., a random bit generator is not required to generate this value, making it acceptable for implementations that do not include a random bit generator).

3.3.1.4   RSA

The RSA algorithm is **approved** for the generation and verification of digital signatures in FIPS 186 and specified in PKCS 1 and RFC 8017. FIPS 186 includes restrictions on the use of RSA to generate digital signatures, methods to generate RSA key pairs, and defines the key lengths to be used for secure interoperability. Additional discussions of RSA key pair generation are included in SP 800-56B.[56]

---

[56] SP 800-56B, *Recommendation for Pair-Wise Key-Establishment Schemes Using Integer Factorization Cryptography.*

3.3.2 Key-Establishment Schemes

Asymmetric key-establishment schemes are used to set up keys to be used between communicating entities. A scheme is a set of transformations (i.e., cryptographic operations) that provide a cryptographic service – a key-establishment service, in this case; a scheme is used in a protocol that actually performs the communication needed for the key-establishment process.

Two classes of asymmetric schemes have been **approved** that are based on hard mathematical problems: discrete-log-based schemes and integer factorization schemes.

3.3.2.1 Diffie–Hellman and MQV

SP 800-56A specifies key-establishment schemes that use discrete-logarithm-based algorithms. These schemes are specified using either finite-field math (the form of math that most of us use) or elliptic curve math.

Two algorithms have been approved for key agreement: Diffie–Hellman (DH) and MQV.[57] The use of these algorithms for key agreement is specified in SP 800-56A and discussed in Section 5.3.3.

For finite-field DH and MQV, SP 800-56A specifies that the domain parameters be selected from one of the domain-parameter groups listed in SP 800-56A[58] or be generated in the same manner as the domain parameters for DSA (see FIPS 186). The listed groups are the preferred domain parameters to be used. Key pairs are generated in the same manner as for DSA (see FIPS 186).

For elliptic-curve DH and MQV, methods for generating key pairs are specified in FIPS 186 using the same methods used to generate ECDSA key pairs. Recommended elliptic curves for DH and MQV key-establishment are provided in SP 800-186, along with specifications for generating new curves.

3.3.2.2 RSA

RSA can be used for key establishment, as well as for the generation and verification of digital signatures. Its use for key establishment is specified in SP 800-56B. That publication specifies **approved** methods for both key agreement and key transport (see Section 5.3 for further information on key establishment, key agreement, and key transport).

Since RSA can be used for both key establishment and the generation of digital signatures, it is important that the same keys not be used for both purposes (see Section 5.2 of SP 800-57, Part 1 for a discussion on key usage).

3.4 Algorithm Security Strength

The security strength of a cryptographic algorithm is measured by an attacker's difficulty in breaking the algorithm. Breaking a cryptographic algorithm can be defined as defeating some aspect of the protection that the algorithm is intended to provide. For example, a

---

[57] Menezes–Qu–Vanstone.

[58] These groups have been specified in RFC 3526 and RFC 7919.

block-cipher encryption algorithm that is used to protect the confidentiality of data is broken if, with an acceptable amount of work, it is possible to determine the value of its key or to recover the plaintext from the ciphertext without knowledge of the key.

SP 800-57, Part 1 provides the current estimates for the security strengths that can be provided by the **approved** cryptographic algorithms; these strengths have been determined with respect to specific key lengths.

The **approved** security strengths for federal applications are 112, 128, 192, and 256 bits. Note that a security strength of 80 bits was previously approved as well. Since it is no longer considered to provide adequate protection, the use of algorithms and keys providing a security strength of 80 bits are **no longer approved** for applying cryptographic protection (e.g., encrypting data). However, algorithms and keys providing 80 bits of strength can be used for processing data that was previously protected at that strength (e.g., for decryption), although some risk must be accepted.

Appropriate algorithms, key lengths, and key generation and handling methods need to be used to actually support those security strengths.

3.5   Algorithm Lifetime

Over time, algorithms may be successfully attacked so that the algorithm no longer provides the desired protection; DES and TDEA are examples of such algorithms (see Sections 3.2.1.1 and 3.2.1.2, respectively). The attack could be on the algorithm itself or on the algorithm with a specific key length. In the latter case, the use of a longer key for algorithms other than DES and TDEA[59] may prevent a successful attack or at least delay it for a period of time.

When selecting the algorithms and key lengths to be used for an application, the length of time for which the data needs to be protected **should** be taken into account so that a suitable algorithm and key length are used. SP 800-57, Part 1 provides a current estimate of the time frames during which the **approved** algorithms and key lengths are considered to be secure. The algorithms and key lengths used for cryptographic protection need to fall within the estimated time frame. However, these estimates are just that – estimates. It is possible that an advance in technology (e.g., the use of quantum computers and algorithms) or cryptanalysis could occur prior to the end date of that time frame. It is often the case that these advances are initially impractical or limited in their threat. It is recommended that an organization have a transition strategy for addressing this problem if it occurs, including assessing the risk for the compromise of the organization's data and transitioning to a new algorithm or key length if appropriate.

---

[59] DES and TDEA have only one defined key length.

4   Cryptographic Services

All sensitive information requires integrity protection, and confidentiality protection may
be required as well. This section discusses the cryptographic services that can be provided
for the protection of sensitive data other than keys. These services include data
confidentiality, data integrity authentication, identity authentication, source authentication,
and support for non-repudiation. The protection and management of the keys used while
providing these cryptographic services are discussed in Section 5.

Ideally, cryptographic services would be provided using as few algorithms as possible. For
example, AES could be used to provide confidentiality (Section 4.1), data integrity
authentication (Section 4.2), key wrapping (Section 5.3.5), and the basis for a random bit
generator (see Section 4.4). However, this may not be as practical as it first appears, as
other algorithms may also be available that are needed for different applications and that
provide other security properties.

A discussion on combining confidentiality and authentication in a single block-cipher
mode of operation is provided in Section 4.3.

4.1   Data Confidentiality

Encryption is used to provide confidentiality for data. The unprotected form of the data is
called plaintext. Encryption transforms the plaintext data into ciphertext, and ciphertext
can be transformed back into plaintext using decryption. Data encryption and decryption
are generally provided using symmetric-key block cipher algorithms. AES is **approved** for
data encryption using all three key sizes (see Section 3.2.1.4). While the use of three-key
TDEA is still allowed for encryption, its use has been deprecated (see Section 3.2.1.2 and
SP 800-131A).

Decryption of the ciphertext is performed using the algorithm and key that were used to
encrypt the plaintext. Unauthorized recipients of the ciphertext who know the
cryptographic algorithm but do not have the correct key should not be able to decrypt the
ciphertext. However, anyone who has the key and the cryptographic algorithm can easily
decrypt the ciphertext and obtain the original plaintext.

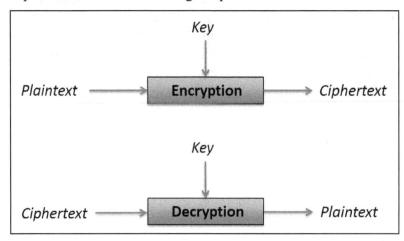

Figure 2: Encryption and Decryption

Figure 2 depicts the encryption and decryption processes. The plaintext and a key are used by the encryption process to produce the ciphertext. To decrypt, the ciphertext and the same key are used by the decryption process to recover the plaintext data.

Note that asymmetric-key algorithms could also be used to encrypt and decrypt data, but because these algorithms are slow in comparison to block cipher algorithms, they are not normally used to encrypt and decrypt general data; they can, however, be used to protect keys, as discussed in Section 5.

As discussed in Section 3.2.1.5, data encryption is performed using a block cipher algorithm and a mode of operation. The **approved** modes of operation for encryption are specified in:

- SP 800-38A for AES and TDEA: the Electronic Codebook (ECB), Cipher Block Chaining (CBC), Cipher Feedback (CFB), Counter (CTR), and Output Feedback (OFB) modes,

- SP 800-38E for AES: the XTS-AES mode (for protecting the confidentiality of data on storage devices only), and

- SP 800-38G for AES: the FF1 and FF3 modes for Format Preserving Encryption (FPE).

Additional modes that provide both confidentiality and authentication (as discussed in Section 4.2) are discussed in Section 4.3.

4.2　　Data Integrity, Identity Authentication, and Source Authentication

Data integrity (often referred to as simply *integrity*) is concerned with whether or not data has changed between two specified times (e.g., between the time when the data was created, stored, and/or transmitted and the time when it was retrieved and/or received). While data integrity cannot be guaranteed, the use of data integrity codes provides a means to detect changes with a high probability. A data integrity code is computed on data when it is created, before storage or before transmission, and computed again when the data is retrieved or received. Verification that these computations agree provides a measure of assurance of data integrity. In cryptographic literature, this process is called *message* (or data) *authentication*, and the integrity code is often a MAC or digital signature.

Identity authentication (often referred to as simply *authentication*) is used to provide assurance of the identity of an entity interacting with a system. The authentication process usually requires that the entity produce some proof of its identity (e.g., using a token, fingerprint, PIN, or some combination thereof) before access to some data or resource can be granted.

Source authentication is a process used to provide assurance of the source of information that is transmitted or stored. Depending on the method used, source authentication could also support non-repudiation (i.e., whether a third party, such as a legal entity, can be convinced about who was the source of the information).[60]

Cryptography can be used to provide these services, but the same algorithm may not provide all of them. Hash functions, as discussed in Section 4.2.1, can be used to provide some assurance of data integrity. Message Authentication Code (MAC) algorithms, as discussed in Section 4.2.2, can provide both data integrity and source authentication services. Digital signature algorithms can be used to provide data integrity authentication, identity authentication, and source authentication services, as well as support for non-repudiation but at a higher performance cost (see Section 4.2.3).

4.2.1 Hash Functions

A hash function is used to generate a hash value that can provide some assurance of the integrity of the data over which the hash value is generated. However, if a hash function is used alone (e.g., without the use of a secret key, as is required for HMAC, or in conjunction with the generation of digital signatures), there is no assurance that the data has not been altered by an adversary and a new hash value computed. Therefore, the use of a hash function alone for providing integrity protection is not recommended unless there is a very low risk of this scenario (e.g., when data is provided by a trusted source, and the hash value is used only to determine changes that may occur because of a degraded transmission medium).

4.2.2 Message Authentication Code Algorithms

A Message Authentication Code algorithm and a cryptographic key are used to generate a message authentication code (MAC) that can be used to provide assurance of data integrity and source authentication. A MAC is a cryptographic checksum on the data that can provide assurance that the data has not changed or been altered since it was either saved or transmitted. A MAC is generated on data by one entity (say, entity A), and the integrity of the data can be verified by any entity that knows the key used to generate the MAC. If the data is stored with its MAC, and the key is known by entities A, B, and C, then either A, B, or C can retrieve the data and MAC from storage and verify its integrity (i.e., verify that the data has not been modified while in storage).

If entity A sends the data and MAC to another entity that knows the key (e.g., entity B), the receiver (B) can verify that the data has not been modified during transmission. If only A and B know the key, then entity B (the receiver) also knows that only entity A can have sent the data (i.e., entity A is the source of the data). However, if the data and MAC are sent to more than one entity (i.e., multiple receivers know the key, such as entities B and C), each receiver can verify the integrity of the received data, but assurance of the source cannot be obtained (e.g., from entity B's perspective as a receiver, either entity A or entity B could be the source, since both know the key). Note that this may be acceptable for some applications.

---

[60] A real determination of non-repudiation is a legal decision with many aspects to be considered. Cryptographic mechanisms can only be used as one element in this decision (i.e., a digital signature can only be used to support a non-repudiation decision).

MACs are used to detect data modifications that occur between the initial generation of the MAC and the verification of the received or retrieved MAC. They do not detect errors that occur before the MAC is originally generated. The use of MACs to provide data integrity and source authentication depends on limiting knowledge of the secret key to only those parties generating the MAC and those intended to retrieve or receive it. Since a MAC key is shared among a community of users (e.g., two or more parties), only those parties sharing the key can compute a correct MAC on given data.

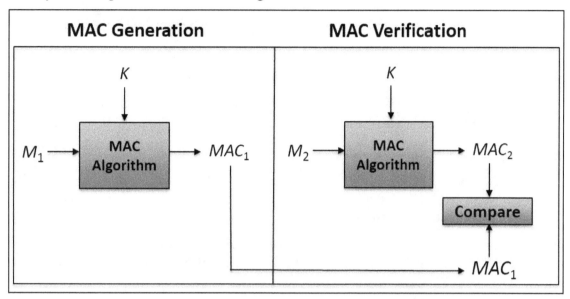

Figure 3: Message Authentication and Verification

Figure 3 depicts the use of message authentication codes:

- A message authentication code (MAC_1) is computed on data (M_1) using a key (K). M_1 and MAC_1 are then saved or transmitted.

- At a later time, the integrity of the saved or received data is checked. Consider the saved or received data as M_2 and the saved or received message authentication code as MAC_1.

- Compute a message authentication code on M_2 using the same key (K), and label that message authentication code as MAC_2.

- If $MAC_1 = MAC_2$, then it can be assumed that M_2 (the saved or retrieved data) is the same as the data on which MAC_1 was computed (M_1) (i.e., $M_1 = M_2$).

Assurance of data integrity is frequently provided using non-cryptographic techniques known as error detection codes. However, these codes can be altered by an adversary to the adversary's benefit. The use of an **approved** cryptographic mechanism, such as a MAC, addresses this problem. That is, the assurance of integrity provided by a MAC is based on the assumption that it is not likely that anyone could correctly generate a MAC without knowing the cryptographic key. An adversary without knowledge of the key will not be able to modify data and then generate a verifiable MAC on the modified data. It is therefore crucial that MAC keys be kept secret.

Two types of algorithms for computing a MAC have been **approved** for Federal
Government use: MAC algorithms that are based on symmetric-key block cipher
algorithms and MAC algorithms that are based on hash or hash-related functions.

4.2.2.1   MACs Based on Block Cipher Algorithms

The SP 800-38 series of publications includes modes for the generation of MACs:

- SP 800-38B defines the CMAC mode for computing a MAC using the AES and
  TDEA block-cipher algorithms; see Section 3.2.1.2 about the deprecated use of
  TDEA.

- SP 800-38D defines the GMAC mode for the computation of a MAC using AES.

- Modes providing both confidentiality (i.e., encryption) and authentication (i.e.,
  computing a MAC) in a single operation are also defined (see Section 4.3).

4.2.2.2   MACs Based on Hash Functions

FIPS 198 defines a MAC (HMAC) that uses a cryptographic hash function in combination
with a secret key. HMAC must be used with an **approved** cryptographic hash function (see
Section 4.2.1). The security associated with the use of HMAC is discussed in SP 800-107.[61]

SP 800-185 defines another MAC algorithm (KMAC) that is based on the extendable
output function specified in FIPS 202. Two variations of KMAC have been specified:
KMAC 128 and KMAC256. Their security is discussed in SP 800-185.

4.2.3   Digital Signature Algorithms

A digital signature algorithm is used with a pair of keys – a private key and a public key –
to generate and verify digital signatures. The private key is used to generate signatures and
must be known only by the signer (the key-pair owner); the public key is used to verify the
signatures. Because of the design of the algorithm and the methods for generating key pairs,
the public key cannot efficiently be used to determine the private key. Since two keys are
required for the generation and verification process, digital signature algorithms are
classified as asymmetric-key algorithms.

A digital signature is represented in a computer as a string of bits and is an electronic
analogue of a hand-written signature that can be verified by anyone with access to the
public key. The signature can be used to provide data integrity authentication, identity
authentication, source authentication, and to support non-repudiation.

Each signer possesses a private and public key pair. Signature generation (with a verifiable
digital signature) can be performed only by the party that has access to the private key.
Anyone that knows the public key can verify the signature by employing the associated
public key. The security of a digital-signature system is dependent on maintaining the
secrecy of the signer's private key. Therefore, signers must guard against the unauthorized
disclosure of their private keys.

---

[61] SP 800-107, *Recommendation for Applications Using Approved Hash Algorithms*.

Digital signatures offer protection that is not available by using alternative signature techniques. One such alternative is a digitized signature. A digitized signature is generated by converting a visual form of a handwritten signature to an electronic image (e.g., by scanning it into a computer). Although a digitized signature resembles its handwritten counterpart when printed, it does not provide the same protection as a digital signature. Digitized signatures can be forged or duplicated, and can be appended to other electronic data; digitized signatures also cannot be used to determine if information has been altered after it is signed. Digital signatures, however, are computed on each message using a private key known only by the signer. Each different message signed by the signer will have a different digital signature. Even small changes to the message will result in a different signature. If an adversary does not know the private key, the adversary cannot generate a valid signature (i.e., a signature that can be verified using the public key that corresponds to the private key used to generate the signature).

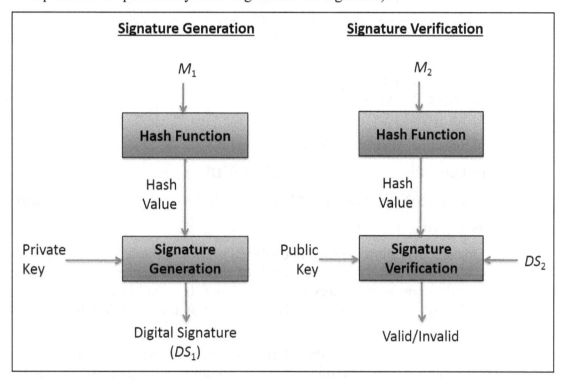

Figure 4: Digital Signature Generation and Verification

Figure 4 depicts the generation and verification of digital signatures. A digital signature algorithm includes a signature generation process and a signature verification process.

a. Signature generation:
1. A hash function (see Section 3.1) is used in the signature generation process to obtain a hash value, which is a condensed version of the data to be signed (i.e., shown as M_1 for signature generation in Figure 4).

2. The hash value is then input to the signature generation process, along with a private key, to generate the digital signature (shown as DS_1 in Figure 4).

3. The digital signature (DS_1) is provided to the verifier along with the data that has been signed (M_1) (i.e., DS_1 and M_1 are either transmitted to an intended receiver(s) or stored for later retrieval).

b. Signature verification: The receiver of the transmitted data and signature (or the entity retrieving the data and signature from storage) verifies the signature as follows.

1. The received/retrieved data (M_2)[62] is hashed using the same hash function that was used during signature generation to produce another hash value. (Note that if the data was modified during transmission or storage, the newly computed hash value will not be the same as the hash value computed during signature generation (in step a.1)).

2. The newly computed hash value and the received/retrieved signature (DS_2)[63] are input to the signature verification process along with the signer's public key. The output of this process is an indication of whether or not the signature is valid or invalid for the received/retrieved data (M_2).

FIPS 186 specifies methods for generating and verifying digital signatures using asymmetric (public-key) cryptography. Four digital signature algorithms are included in FIPS 186-4:

- Digital Signature Algorithm (DSA) (see Section 3.3.1.1),

- Elliptic Curve Digital Signature Algorithm (ECDSA) (see Section 3.3.1.2),

- Edwards-Curve Digital Signature Algorithm (EdDSA) (see Section 3.3.1.3), and

- RSA (see Section 3.3.1.4).

The digital signature algorithms are used in conjunction with the hash functions specified in FIPS 180, FIPS 202, and SP 800-185. Each of these algorithms requires obtaining assurances about the domain parameters and/or keys used, as discussed in Section 3.3; SP 800-89[64] provides methods for obtaining these required assurances when using digital signatures.

In many cases, determining when a digital signature was generated is important. For example, it may be important to determine whether a document was signed before a certain date (e.g., which of two wills was signed closest to and prior to the date that a person died). SP 800-102[65] provides guidance on establishing when a digital signature was generated.

---

[62] Since a transmission/storage error may have occurred, or a malicious adversary may have modified the data while in transit/storage, the received/retrieved data may be different than the data that was hashed during signature generation (see step a.1). Therefore, the received/retrieved data is called M_2 rather than M_1.

[63] The signature could also have been modified during transmission/storage. Therefore, DS_2 is used rather than DS_1 (the generated signature from step).

[64] SP 800-89, *Recommendation for Obtaining Assurances for Digital Signature Applications*.

[65] SP 800-102, *Recommendation for Digital Signature Timeliness*.

4.3   Combining Confidentiality and Authentication in a Block-Cipher Mode of Operation

Confidentiality and authentication can be provided using either two separate block-cipher algorithms (e.g., AES in the CBC mode for encryption and HMAC for authentication) or in a single block-cipher mode of operation. Note that in this discussion, authentication is used to obtain both an assurance of data integrity and of the source of the data that has been cryptographically protected.

If encryption and authentication are performed as two separate operations (see Sections 4.1 and 4.2, respectively), two distinct keys are required. If care is not taken in performing these operations (e.g., performing the operations in the right order), vulnerabilities can be introduced that may allow attacks. Well-vetted, standardized protocols and constructions **should** be used when encryption and authentication are performed separately.

An alternative is to use modes that both encrypt and authenticate in a single operation using a single key; such a mode is called an "authenticated-encryption" mode. Using such modes requires fewer keys and is generally faster than using two separate operations. Two authenticated-encryption modes have been defined for AES (no such mode has been defined for TDEA):

- SP 800-38C specifies the CCM mode, and

- SP 800-38D defines the Galois/Counter mode (GCM).

4.4   Random Bit Generation

Cryptography and security applications make extensive use of random numbers and random bits. For cryptography, random values are needed to generate cryptographic keys. The term "entropy" is used to describe the amount of randomness in a value, and the amount of entropy determines how hard it is to guess that value.

There are two classes of random bit generators (RBGs): Non-Deterministic Random Bit Generators (NRBGs), sometimes called true random number (or bit) generators, and Deterministic Random Bit Generators (DRBGs), sometimes called pseudorandom bit (or number) generators. Each RBG is dependent on the use of an entropy source to provide unpredictable bits that are outside of human control; these bits are acquired from some physical source, such as thermal noise, ring oscillators, or hard-drive seek times. An NRBG is dependent on the availability of new, unused entropy bits produced by the entropy source for every NRBG output. A DRBG is initially "seeded" with entropy produced by an entropy source or using an **approved** method that depends on an entropy source (e.g., an NRBG); depending on the application, the DRBG may or may not receive additional entropy during operation (e.g., by being reseeded).

Several publications have been developed or are currently under development for random-bit generation:

- SP 800-90A specifies **approved** DRBG algorithms based on the use of hash functions and block-cipher algorithms; DRBGs must be initialized from a randomness source (e.g., an entropy source or an NRBG) that provides sufficient entropy for the security strength(s) to be supported by the DRBG.

- SP 800-90B[66] discusses entropy sources, including the health tests needed to determine that the entropy source has not failed and tests for the validation of the entropy sources by an accredited lab.

- SP 800-90C[67] provides constructions for the design and implementation of NRBGs and DRBGs from the algorithms in SP 800-90A and the entropy sources designed in accordance with SP 800-90B. Note that the NRBGs are constructed to include a DRBG algorithm from SP 800-90A to provide a fallback capability if an entropy source failure is not immediately detected.

- SP 800-22[68] discusses some aspects of selecting and testing random and pseudorandom number generators. This document includes some criteria for characterizing and selecting appropriate generators, discusses statistical testing and its relation to cryptanalysis, and provides some recommended statistical tests. These tests may be useful as a first step in determining whether or not a generator is suitable for a particular cryptographic application. However, for federal applications, the RBGs must be validated for compliance to FIPS 140 and the appropriate parts of SP 800-90.

4.5   Symmetric vs. Asymmetric Cryptography

As discussed in Sections 3.2 and 3.3, when large numbers of cryptographic relationships are required, the number of initial symmetric keys that will be required may be significantly larger than the number of public/private key pairs required.

However, a primary advantage of symmetric-key cryptography is speed. Symmetric-key algorithms are generally significantly faster than asymmetric-key algorithms, and the keys are shorter in length for the same security strength; the key length may be an important consideration if memory for storing the keys or the bandwidth for transporting the keys is limited. In addition, advances in cryptanalysis and computational efficiency have tended to reduce the level of protection provided by public-key cryptography more rapidly than that provided by symmetric-key cryptography. Also, in a potential post-quantum world, the currently approved asymmetric-key algorithms will not provide adequate protection.

Since asymmetric-key (i.e., public-key) cryptography requires fewer keys overall, and symmetric-key cryptography is significantly faster, a hybrid approach is often used whereby asymmetric-key algorithms are used for the generation and verification of digital signatures and for initial key establishment, while symmetric-key algorithms are used for all other purposes (e.g., encryption), especially those involving the protection of large amounts of data and for key distribution when entities share an already established symmetric key (e.g., established using manual distribution methods or asymmetric key-establishment methods). For example, an asymmetric-key system can be used to establish a symmetric key via a key-agreement or key-transport process (see Sections 5.3.3 and

---

[66] SP 800-90B, *Recommendation for the Entropy Sources Used for Random Bit Generation.*

[67] SP 800-90C, *Recommendation for Random Bit Generator (RBG) Constructions.*

[68] SP 800-22, *A Statistical Test Suite for Random and Pseudorandom Number Generators for Cryptographic Applications.*

5.3.4, respectively), after which the symmetric key is used to encrypt files or messages or to distribute other keys.

In some situations, asymmetric-key cryptography is not necessary, and symmetric-key cryptography alone is sufficient. This includes environments where secure symmetric-key establishment can take place using symmetric keys already shared between entities, environments where a single authority knows and manages all the keys, and in single-user environments.

In general, asymmetric-key cryptography is best suited for an open, multi-user environment. However, with the impending availability of quantum computing, the current asymmetric algorithms will become vulnerable to attacks (see the note in Section 3.3).

5   Key Management

The proper management of cryptographic keys is essential to the effective use of cryptography for security. Keys are analogous to the combination of a safe. If a safe combination becomes known by an adversary, that safe provides no security against penetration by that adversary. Similarly, poor key management may easily compromise strong algorithms. Ultimately, the security of information protected by cryptography directly depends on the strength of the keys, the effectiveness of the mechanisms and protocols associated with the keys, and the protection afforded to all key information – the keying material and all information associated with that keying material (i.e., the key's metadata). See SP 800-57, Part 1 for a suggested list of the metadata that may be appropriate.

All key information needs to be protected against modification (i.e., the integrity needs to be preserved), and secret and private keys (i.e., keys used by symmetric and asymmetric algorithms, respectively) and any secret metadata need to be protected against unauthorized disclosure (i.e., their confidentiality needs to be maintained).

Key management provides the foundation for the secure generation, storage, distribution/establishment, use, and destruction of keys and is essential at all phases of a key's life. If a strong algorithm is used to encrypt data using keys that are properly generated, then the protection of that data can subsequently be reduced to just protecting the key information (i.e. the security of information protected by cryptography directly depends on the protection afforded the key information). Therefore, a Cryptographic Key Management System (CKMS) is required for managing keys and the information associated with them.

5.1   General Key Management Guidance

Several publications have been developed to provide general key-management guidance: SP 800-57 (see Section 5.1.1), FIPS 140 (see Section 5.1.2), and SP 800-131A (see Section 5.1.3).

5.1.1   Recommendation for Key Management

SP 800-57 provides general guidance on the management of cryptographic keys and associated information: their generation, use, and eventual destruction. Related topics – such as algorithm selection, appropriate key size, and cryptographic policy – are also included in SP 800-57, which consists of three parts:

1. SP 800-57, Part 1, *General Guidance*, contains basic key-management guidance, including

   - Protection required for keying material;

   - Key life-cycle responsibilities;

   - Key backup, archiving, and recovery;

   - Changing keys;

   - Cryptoperiods (i.e., the appropriate lengths of time that keys are to be used);

- Accountability and auditing;

- Key inventories;

- Contingency planning; and

- Key compromise recovery (e.g., by generating new keys).

Federal agencies have a variety of information that they have determined to require cryptographic protection; the sensitivity of the information and the periods of time that the protection is required also vary. To this end, NIST has established four security strengths for the protection of information: 112, 128, 192, and 256 bits.[69] These security strengths have been assigned to the **approved** cryptographic algorithms and key sizes, and dates have been projected during which the use of these algorithms and key sizes is anticipated to be secure. For further information, see SP 800-131A (discussed in Section 5.1.3).

Agencies need to determine the length of time that cryptographic protection is required before selecting an algorithm and key size with the appropriate security strength.

Note that SP 800-57, Part 1 is updated whenever the guidance provided therein is no longer valid (e.g., an algorithm no longer provides adequate security).

2. SP 800-57, Part 2, *Best Practices for Key Management Organization*:

- Identifies the concepts, functions, and elements common to effective systems for the management of symmetric and asymmetric keys;
- Identifies the security-planning requirements and documentation necessary for effective institutional key management;
- Describes key-management specification requirements;
- Describes cryptographic key-management policy documentation that is needed by organizations that use cryptography; and
- Describes key-management practice-statement requirements.

3. SP 800-57, Part 3, *Application-Specific Key Management Guidance*, addresses the key-management issues associated with currently available cryptographic mechanisms, such as the Public Key Infrastructure (PKI), Internet Protocol Security (IPsec), Secure/Multipart Internet Mail Extensions (S/MIME), Kerberos, Over-the-Air Rekeying (OTAR), Domain Name System Security Extensions (DNSSEC), Encrypted File Systems, and the Secure Shell (SSH) protocol.

Specific guidance is provided regarding

- The recommended and/or allowable algorithm suites and key sizes,

- Recommendations for the use of the mechanism in its current form for the protection of Federal Government information, and

---

[69] A fifth security strength (i.e., 80 bits of security) was acceptable for applying cryptographic protection (e.g., encryption) prior to 2014. However, this strength is no longer adequate.

- Security considerations that may affect the effectiveness of key-management processes and the cryptographic mechanisms using keys that are generated and managed by those key-management processes.

Note that the Transport Layer Security (TLS) protocol was included in the original version of this document; however, Part 3 now references a separate document that discusses TLS (see SP 800-52).[70]

New key-management techniques and mechanisms are constantly being developed, and existing key-management mechanisms and techniques are constantly being refined. While the security-guidance information contained in Part 3 will be updated as mechanisms and techniques evolve, new products and technical specifications can always be expected that are not reflected in the current version of the document. Therefore, the context provided may include status information, such as version numbers or implementation status at the time that the document was last revised.

5.1.2 Security Requirements for Cryptographic Modules

FIPS 140 provides minimum security requirements for cryptographic modules that embody or support cryptography in federal information systems. A cryptographic module performs the actual cryptographic computations for a security system protecting sensitive information. The security requirements cover areas related to the secure design and implementation of a cryptographic module, including the module specification; cryptographic module ports and interfaces; roles, services, and authentication; finite-state models; physical security; the operational environment; cryptographic key management; electromagnetic interference/electromagnetic compatibility (EMI/EMC); self-tests; design assurance; and the mitigation of attacks.

FIPS 140 is applicable to all federal agencies that use cryptography to protect sensitive information in computer and telecommunications systems. Further information about FIPS 140 and the validation of cryptographic modules is available at https://csrc.nist.gov/Projects/Cryptographic-Module-Validation-Program.

5.1.3 Transitions to New Cryptographic Algorithms and Key Lengths

With the development and publication of SP 800-57, Part 1, NIST provided recommendations for transitioning to new cryptographic algorithms and key lengths because of algorithm breaks or the availability of more powerful computers that could be used to efficiently search for cryptographic keys. SP 800-131A was developed to provide more specific guidance for such transitions. Each algorithm and service is addressed in SP 800-131A, indicating whether its use is acceptable,[71] deprecated,[72] allowed only for legacy applications,[73] or disallowed.

---

[70] SP 800-52, *Guidelines for the Selection, Configuration, and Use of Transport Layer Security (TLS) Implementations.*

[71] No security risk is known at present.

[72] The use of the algorithm and key length is allowed, but the user must accept some risk.

[73] The algorithm and key length may be used to process already-protected information, but there may be a risk in doing so.

Note that SP 800-131A is updated when necessary (e.g., to provide a transition schedule for an algorithm that no longer provides adequate security).

5.2 Cryptographic Key Management Systems

Several publications have been developed for the development of key-management systems: SP 800-130[74] (see Section 5.2.1), SP 800-152[75] (see Section 5.2.2), and documents relating to the Public Key Infrastructure used for asymmetric-key cryptography (see Section 5.2.3).

A Cryptographic Key Management System (CKMS) includes policies, procedures, components, and devices that are used to protect, manage, and distribute key information. A CKMS includes all devices or subsystems that can access a key or the other information associated with it. The devices could be computers, cell phones, tablets, or other smart devices, such as cars, alarm systems, or even refrigerators.

5.2.1 Key Management Framework

SP 800-130 contains topics that **should** be considered by a CKMS designer when developing a CKMS design specification. Topics include security policies, cryptographic keys and metadata, interoperability and transitioning, security controls, testing and system assurances, disaster recovery, and security assessments.

For each topic, SP 800-130 specifies one or more documentation requirements that need to be addressed by the designer. SP 800-130 is intended to assist in

- The definition of the CKMS design by requiring the specification of significant CKMS capabilities,

- Encouraging CKMS designers to consider the factors needed in a comprehensive CKMS,

- Logically comparing different CKMSs and their capabilities,

- Performing security assessments by requiring the specification of implemented and supported CKMS capabilities, and

- Forming the basis for the development of Profiles that specify the specific requirements for the CKMS to be used by an organization.

5.2.2 Key Management System Profile

SP 800-152 contains requirements for the design, implementation, procurement, installation, configuration, management, operation, and use of a CKMS by and for U.S. federal organizations and their contractors. The Profile is based on SP 800-130 (see Section 5.2.1). SP 800-152 specifies requirements, makes recommendations for federal organizations having special security needs and desiring to augment the base security and key-management services, and suggests additional features that may be desirable to implement and use.

---

[74] SP 800-130, *A Framework for Designing Cryptographic Key Management Systems.*

[75] SP 800-152, *A Profile for U. S. Federal Cryptographic Key Management Systems (CKMS).*

In addition to providing design requirements to be incorporated into a CKMS design, SP 800-152 provides requirements for a Federal CKMS (FCKMS) to be operated by a service provider that may be a federal agency or a third party operating an FCKMS under contract for one or more federal agencies and their contractors.

This Profile is intended to

- Assist CKMS designers and implementers in supporting appropriate cryptographic algorithms and keys, selecting the metadata associated with the keys, and selecting protocols for protecting sensitive U.S. federal computing applications and data;

- Establish requirements for testing, procurement, installation, configuration, administration, operation, maintenance, and usage of the FCKMS;

- Facilitate an easy comparison of one CKMS with another by analyzing their designs and implementations in order to understand how each meets the Framework (i.e., SP 800-130) and Profile (e.g., SP 800-152) requirements; and

- Assist in understanding what is needed to evaluate, procure, install, configure, administer, operate, and use an FCKMS that manages the key information that is used to protect sensitive and valuable data obtained, processed, stored, and used by U.S. federal organizations and their contractors.

5.2.3 Public Key Infrastructure

A PKI is a security infrastructure that creates and manages public-key certificates to facilitate the use of public-key (i.e., asymmetric-key) cryptography. To achieve this goal, a PKI needs to perform two basic tasks:

1. Generate and provide public key certificates that bind public keys to the identifier associated with the owner of the corresponding private key[76] and to other required information *after* validating the accuracy of the information to be bound; and

2. Maintain and provide certificate-status information for unexpired and revoked certificates.

Two types of certificates are commonly used: certificates used to provide the public keys that are used to verify digital signatures and certificates used to provide the public keys used for key establishment. Each certificate associated with digital signatures provides the public keys of one of the digital-signature algorithms approved in FIPS 186: DSA, ECDSA, EdDSA, or RSA (see Section 3.3). Certificates that convey the public keys to be used for key establishment may be of two types: those that provide a key-agreement public key (see Section 5.3.3) and those that provide a key-transport public key (see Section 5.3.4). Key-usage bits in a certificate indicate the purpose for which the public key is intended to be used.

As discussed in Section 3.3, public keys can be made available to anyone. However, a private key must be kept secret and used only by the entity that owns and is authorized to use the private key. An entity may be a person, organization, device, or process, including

---

[76] The identifier could be a publicly known identifier associated with the owner (e.g., the owner's personal name) or an alias or pseudonym used to represent the owner.

network servers. In the case of non-human entities (e.g., devices or processes), one or more humans are assigned as representatives or sponsors of that entity for managing its key information; the representative or sponsor **should not** have access to any secret key information once entered into the system. In this case, the owner of the private key (e.g., a device or process) is not the same as the owner of the certificate (i.e., the human representative or sponsor).

A relying party is an entity that relies on the certificate and the CA that issued the certificate to verify the identity of the certificate owner and the validity of the public key, associated algorithms, and any relevant parameters in the certificate, as well as the private-key owner's possession of the corresponding private key.

The loss or compromise of the private key has the following implications:

- If a private key that is used to generate digital signatures is lost, the owner can no longer generate digital signatures. Some policies may permit backup copies of the private key to be maintained for continuity of operations, but this is not encouraged so an alternative is to simply generate new key pairs and certificates.

- If the private key used to generate digital signatures is compromised, relying parties can no longer trust the digital signatures generated using that private key (e.g., someone may be using the signature to provide false information).

- If a private key used for key establishment is lost (e.g., a key used for key transport or key agreement), then further key establishment processes cannot be accomplished until the key is recovered or replaced. If the key is needed to recover data protected by the key, then that data is lost unless the key can be recovered. For example, if the key is used to transport a decryption key for encrypted data, and the key is lost, then the encrypted data cannot be decrypted. To ensure that access to critical data is not lost, PKIs often backup the private key-establishment key for possible recovery.

- If a private key used for key establishment is compromised, then any transactions involving that key cannot be trusted (e.g., someone other than the true owner of the private key may be attempting to enter into a supposedly "secure" transaction for some illicit purpose).

5.2.3.1 PKI Components, Relying Parties, and Their Responsibilities

For scalability, PKIs are usually implemented with a set of complementary components, each focused on specific aspects of the PKI process. The main PKI tasks are assigned to the following logical components; other components are also used to support the PKI but are not discussed here (see SP 800-32[77] for further discussion).

- *Certification authorities* (CAs) generate certificates and certificate-status information.

---

[77] SP 800-32, *Introduction to Public Key Technology and the Federal PKI Infrastructure.*

- *Registration authorities* (RAs) verify the identity of users applying for a certificate[78] and authenticate other information to be included in the certificate.

In general, a PKI operates as follows:

1. An application for a certificate is presented to an RA.

2. The RA a) verifies the identity of the applicant and the authorization of the applicant to obtain a certificate, b) verifies the information to be inserted in the certificate, and c) verifies that the applicant has the private key corresponding to the public key to be included in the certificate. The correctness of this information is the linchpin on which the security of using certificates is based.

3. If the checks made by the RA in step 2 indicate that the information to be inserted in the certificate is valid, and the identity and authorization of the applicant has been verified, then the RA sends the public key and other relevant information to the CA to request that a certificate be generated.

4. The security of the certificate generation process requires that the CA only generate certificates for RAs that it trusts. Upon receiving the certificate request from a trusted RA, the CA creates a digital certificate, makes the certificate available to the RA and/or the applicant, and deposits the certificate in a repository. The RA or CA **should** also create an inventory of all certificates.

5. When a relying party interacts with another entity that has a public-key certificate, the relying party needs to obtain the other entity's certificate either directly from the other entity or from the repository where it is stored. After acquiring the certificate, the relying party verifies the signature on the certificate. Assuming that the certificate is "good," then the relying party can proceed safely with its interaction with the public key owner.

Most of the interaction involved with using a certificate is transparent to the user (i.e., the relying party). However, a user or a system administrator may be responsible for obtaining and installing a certificate. Thereafter, an application (e.g., a browser) uses the certificate to interact with other entities, and the user may not be aware of these actions. An exception might be when a certificate has expired or been revoked, in which case a message may be displayed to indicate this status.

Certificates expire at a predetermined time. In many cases, services are denied when certificates expire. A certificate inventory can be used to identify certificates that are nearing expiration, allowing time to replace these certificates prior to their expiration, thus avoiding service outages. A certificate inventory can also be used to detect the use of algorithms and key lengths that are no longer secure, respond to cryptographic incidents (e.g., a CA compromise), and modify who **should** be contacted for certificate maintenance (e.g., the certificate owner).

Certificates may be revoked prior to the expiration date (e.g., using a Certificate Revocation List that identifies revoked certificates). Certificates can be revoked for a variety of reasons, including the compromise of the private key corresponding to the public

---

[78] The certificate could be for the user or for a device for which the user is authorized to obtain a certificate.

key in the certificate or because the certificate owner leaves the organization. When a certificate has been revoked, a system will quite often display the certificate-revocation message and perhaps include the reason for the revocation. Depending on the application implementation and the revocation reason, the application could disallow further actions or allow the user (i.e., the relying party) to indicate whether to ignore the warning and continue operations or to simply discontinue operations. This warning must not be taken lightly. Ignoring the warning means that the user is accepting the risks associated with doing so. For example, if a warning indicates a compromised digital signature certificate, there is a possibility that someone other than the claimed owner of the certificate actually used the private key corresponding to the public key to sign data. Depending on the data, it may not be prudent to ignore the warning. Users **should** consult with their organizations to determine how to respond to this warning.

5.2.3.2   The Certificate Verification Process

A PKI consists of at least one CA with its subscribers, as shown in Figure 5. Each of the subscribers (e.g., User 1, User 2, and User 3) obtains a certificate containing their public key and other information, which is signed by their CA. All CA subscribers are provided with the public key of the CA.

As a basic example of how this works, suppose that User 3 signs a document and sends the signed document to User 1, who needs to verify the contents and source of the signed document. This is accomplished as follows:

1. User 1 obtains the certificate containing the public key that corresponds to the private key used to sign the document (i.e., User 1 obtains User 3's certificate). Either User 3 supplies that certificate or the certificate is obtained from some other source (e.g., the CA).

2. User 1 verifies User 3's certificate using the CA's public key.

3. User 1 then employs the public key in User 3's certificate to verify the signature on the signed document received from User 3. If the signature is successfully verified, then User 1 knows that User 3 generated the signature, and no unauthorized modifications were made to the document after the signature was generated.

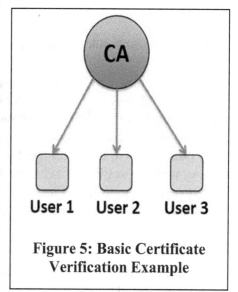

Figure 5: Basic Certificate Verification Example

Other more-complicated scenarios exist when users subscribing to different CAs need to interact using CAs that have cross-certified by signing a certificate for each other. Cross certification is the establishment of a trust relationship between two CAs through the signing of each other's public key in a certificate referred to as a "cross-certificate." Cross-certificates provide a means to create a chain of trust from a single, trusted, root CA to multiple other CAs so that subscribers in one CA domain can interact safely with subscribers in other CA domains (e.g., the subscriber in one CA domain has assurance of the identity of the subscriber in the other domain and assurance of the accurateness of the other information provided by their certificate).

5.2.3.3　CA Certificate Policies and Certificate Practice Statements

Each CA has a Certificate Policy and a Certificate Practices Statement. As defined by ITU[79] Recommendation X.509, a Certificate Policy (CP) is "a named set of rules that indicates the applicability of a certificate to a particular community and/or class of applications with common security requirements." The CP defines the expectations and requirements of the relying party community that will trust the certificates issued by the CAs using that policy. A CP addresses such issues as key generation and storage; certificate generation; key escrow[80] and key recovery; certificate status services, including Certificate Revocation List (CRL) generation and distribution; and system management functions, such as security audits, configuration management, and archiving.

A Certification Practice Statement (CPS) describes how a specific CA issues and manages public-key certificates. The CPS is derived from the applicable CP for the community or application in which the CA participates.

A Federal Public Key Infrastructure (FPKI) has been established for use by the Federal Government (see Section 5.2.3.4 for further information).

Draft NISTIR 7924[81] identifies a baseline set of security controls and practices to support the secure issuance of certificates. NISTIR 7924 is designed to be used as a template and guide for writing a CP for a specific community or a CPS for a specific CA.

5.2.3.4　Federal Public Key Infrastructure

A Federal Public Key Infrastructure (FPKI) provides the Federal Government with a common infrastructure to administer digital certificates and public-private key pairs. The network portion of the FPKI (commonly referred to as the "Bridge") consists of "Principal CAs" designated by various agencies. Each CA within the bridge is cross-certified with every other CA within the bridge, thus establishing a conduit for trust relationships among all CAs within the FPKI. Each Principal CA may also be associated with other CAs that are not part of the bridge. For more information about the FPKI, including its certificate policy and certificate practices statement, see https://www.idmanagement.gov/topics/fpki/.

5.3　Key Establishment

Key establishment is the means by which keys are generated and provided to the entities that are authorized to use them. Scenarios for which key establishment could be performed include the following.

---

[79] International Telecommunication Union.

[80] Saving a key or information that allows the key to be reconstructed so that the key can be recovered if needed (e.g., because of being lost or corrupted).

[81] NISTIR 7924, *Reference Certificate Policy (Second Draft)*.

- A single entity could generate a key (see Section 5.3.1) and use it without providing it to other entities (e.g., for protecting locally stored data).

- A key could be derived from a key that is already shared between two or more entities (see Section 5.3.2).

- Two entities could generate a key using contributions (i.e., data) from each entity using an automated protocol that incorporates a key-agreement scheme (see Section 5.3.3).

- A single entity could generate a key and provide it to one or more other entities, either by a manual means (e.g., a courier or a face-to-face meeting with the key in either printed or electronic form, such as on a flash drive) or using automated protocols that incorporate a key-transport scheme (see Sections 5.3.4 and 5.3.5).

5.3.1 Key Generation

Cryptographic keys are required by most cryptographic algorithms, the exception being hash functions when not used as a component of another cryptographic process (e.g., HMAC). SP 800-133[82] discusses the generation of the keys to be used with the **approved** cryptographic algorithms.

All keys must be based directly or indirectly on the output of an **approved** Random Bit Generator (RBG) and must be generated within FIPS 140-validated cryptographic modules (see FIPS 140). Any random value required by the module must be generated within a cryptographic module.

SP 800-133 provides guidance on generating a key directly from an RBG and references other publications for additional information required for the generation of keys for specific algorithms.

- FIPS 186 provides rules for the generation of the key pairs to be used for the generation of digital signatures.

- SP 800-108 provides methods for the generation of keys from a pre-shared key (also see Section 5.3.2 below).

- SP 800-56A specifies the rules for the generation of key pairs for Diffie–Hellman and MQV key-agreement schemes (also see Section 5.3.3 below).

- SP 800-56B specifies the rules for the generation of key pairs for RSA key-agreement and key-transport schemes (also see Sections 5.3.3 and 5.3.4 below)

- SP 800-132[83] specifies the rules for the generation of keys from passwords.

5.3.2 Key Derivation

Key derivation is concerned with the generation of a key from secret information, although non-secret information may also be used in the generation process in addition to the secret information. Typically, the secret information is shared among entities that need to derive

---

[82] SP 800-133, *Recommendation for Cryptographic Key Generation*.

[83] SP 800-132, *Recommendation for Password-Based Key Derivation, Part 1: Storage Applications*.

the same key for subsequent interactions. The secret information could be a key that is already shared between the entities (i.e., a pre-shared key) or a shared secret that is derived during a key-agreement scheme (see Section 5.3.3).

SP 800-108 specifies several key-derivation functions that use pre-shared keys. A pre-shared key could have been

- Generated by one entity and provided to one or more other entities by some manual means (e.g., a courier or face-to-face meeting),

- Agreed upon by the entities using an automated key-agreement scheme (see Section 5.3.3), or

- Generated by one entity and provided to another entity using an automated key-transport scheme (see Sections 5.3.4 and 5.3.5).

SP 800-56C and SP 800-135[84] provide methods for deriving keys from the shared secrets generated during key agreement (see Section 5.3.3).

5.3.3 Key Agreement

Key agreement is a key-establishment procedure in which the resultant keying material is a function of information contributed by all participants in the key-agreement process so that no participant can predetermine the value of the resulting keying material independent of the contributions of the other participants. Key agreement is usually performed using automated protocols.

SP 800-56A and SP 800-56B provide several automated pair-wise key-agreement schemes (i.e., key-agreement schemes involving two parties). For each scheme, a shared secret is generated, and keying material is derived from the shared secret using a key-derivation method specified or approved in SP 800-56C.

SP 800-56A and SP 800-56B include variations of key-agreement schemes differing in the number of keys used and whether the keys are long term (i.e., static) or an ephemeral value (e.g., a nonce or a short-term key pair). The key-agreement schemes have two participating entities: an initiator and a responder.

---

[84] SP 800-135, *Recommendation for Existing Application-Specific Key Derivation Functions.*

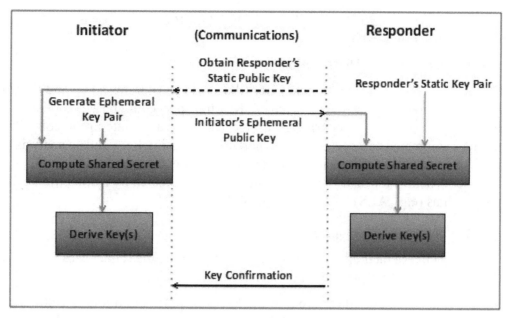

Figure 6: Key Agreement Example

Figure 6 provides an example of a key-agreement scheme where the responder uses a static key pair during the scheme, and the initiator uses an ephemeral key pair. Note that other key-agreement schemes may use other arrangements of key pairs (e.g., each party could use a static key pair, or each party could use an ephemeral key pair). In the example provided in the figure above, the responder's private key is retained by the responder (who is the owner of the key pair), but the responder's public key may be provided to anyone. In this example, the public key is provided to the initiator.

1. The initiator obtains the responder's public key (e.g., from a CA or directly from the responder); for this scheme, this public key is the responder's contribution to the key-agreement process.

2. The initiator then generates a short-term key pair (i.e., an ephemeral key pair) and sends the ephemeral public key to the responder, retaining the ephemeral private key for himself. The ephemeral public key is the initiator's contribution to the key-agreement process for this scheme.

3. Both parties use their own key pair and the other party's public key to generate a shared secret.

4. Both parties then use their copy of the shared secret to derive one or more keys that are (hopefully) identical.

Key confirmation is an optional but highly recommended step that provides assurance that both parties now have the same (identical) key(s) and is shown in Figure 6 for the case that the initiator receives key confirmation from the responder. See SP 800-56A and SP 800-56B for further information.

SP 800-56A specifies Diffie–Hellman (DH) and MQV key-agreement schemes using finite field or elliptic curve mathematics and asymmetric key pairs to generate the shared secret (see Section 3.3.2.1 above), and SP 800-56B specifies two RSA key-agreement schemes (see Section 3.3.2.2 above). SP 800-56A and SP 800-56B also provide an analysis of the security properties provided by each key-agreement scheme.

5.3.4 Key Transport/Key Distribution

Key transport is a method whereby one party (the sender) generates a key and distributes it to one or more other parties (the receiver(s)). Key transport could be accomplished using manual methods (e.g., using a courier) or performed using automated protocols. SP 800-56B provides automated pair-wise key-transport schemes using RSA and an analysis of the security properties provided by each key-transport scheme (see Section 5.3.4.1). SP 800-71[85] provides schemes for distributing keying material protected by symmetric-key block cipher algorithms (e.g., AES) (see Section 5.3.4.2).

5.3.4.1 SP 800-56B Key Transport

SP 800-56B specifies a method for transporting keys whereby the sender uses the receiver's public key to securely transport keying material to the receiver.

Figure 7 provides a simplified example of the key-transport method in SP 800-56B. The receiver must have a key pair that is used during a key-transport transaction. Key transport is accomplished as follows.

The sender:

1. Obtains the public key of the intended receiver,

2. Generates a symmetric key to be transported,

3. Encrypts the symmetric key using the receiver's public key, and

4. Sends the resulting ciphertext key to the receiver.

The receiver:

5. Uses the private key to decrypt the ciphertext key, thus obtaining the original plaintext key.

6. Optionally performs key confirmation; although this step is optional, it is highly recommended to provide assurance that both parties now have the same symmetric key.

---

[85] SP 800-71, *Recommendation for Key Establishment Using Symmetric Block Ciphers*.

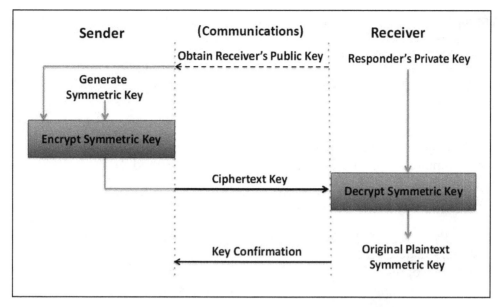

Figure 7: SP 800-56B Key Transport Example

5.3.4.2 SP 800-71 Key Distribution

SP 800-71 addresses the protection of keying material during key distribution using symmetric-key cryptography. Using **approved** key wrapping methods (see Section 5.3.5), techniques are discussed for wrapping keys (i.e., encrypting keys with integrity protection), binding metadata to the keys, and protecting the integrity of the distributed key information.

Several key-distribution architectures are described. These include

- Key distribution among communicating groups that share a key-wrapping key (e.g., pairs of entities),

- The distribution of keys by key generation and distribution centers to their subscribers,

- The use of key-translation centers for the protected distribution of keys generated by one subscriber for distribution to one or more other subscribers, and

- Multiple-center-based environments for key distribution between or among organizational domains.

SP 800-71 does not specify protocols for key distribution but suggests key-distribution communication options and transaction content that **should** be accommodated by key-distribution protocols.

5.3.5 Key Wrapping

Key wrapping is a method used to provide confidentiality and integrity protection for keys (and possibly other information) using a symmetric-key block cipher algorithm and symmetric key-wrapping keys that are known by both the sender and receiver. The wrapped keying material can then be stored or transmitted (i.e., distributed) securely.

Unwrapping the keying material requires the use of the same algorithm and key-wrapping key that was used during the original wrapping process.

Key wrapping differs from simple encryption in that the wrapping process includes both encryption and integrity protection. During the unwrapping process, a method for integrity verification is used to detect accidental or intentional modifications to the wrapped keying material.

SP 800-38F[86] specifies three methods for key wrapping and approves other SP 800-38 modes (or combination of modes). Depending on the method or mode, either AES or TDEA can be used.

5.3.6 Derivation of a Key from a Password

Keys can be derived from passwords. Due to the ease of guessing most passwords, keys derived in this manner are not suitable for most applications. However, SP 800-132 specifies a family of functions that can be used to derive keying material from a password[87] for electronic storage applications (e.g., when encrypting an entire disk drive).

5.4 Key Management Issues

A number of issues need to be addressed for selecting and using a CKMS.

5.4.1 Manual vs. Automated Key Establishment

As discussed in Section 5.3, keys can be established between entities either manually or using automated methods. In many cases, a hybrid approach is used in which an entity generates and manually distributes one or more keys to other entities, and thereafter these keys are used to establish other keys (see SP 800-56A, SP 800-56B, and SP 800-71).

The number of keys to be manually distributed depends on the type of cryptography to be used (i.e., symmetric or asymmetric methods) and must be considered when selecting the capabilities required of a CKMS.

5.4.2 Selecting and Operating a CKMS

A CKMS could be designed, implemented, and operated by the organization that will use it. The organization could operate a CKMS procured from a vendor, or an organization could procure the services of a third party that procures a CKMS from a vendor. Whichever choice is made, the organization needs to make sure that the CKMS that is used provides the protections that are required for the organization's information. SP 800-130 and SP 800-152 discuss the considerations that need to be addressed by a federal organization, including the scalability of the CKMS and the metadata to be associated with the keys.

5.4.3 Storing and Protecting Keys

Keys can be stored in a number of places and protected in a variety of ways. They could be stored in a safe. They could be present only in a validated cryptographic module where the module itself might adequately protect the keys, depending on its design. Keys could also be stored on electronic media, such as a flash drive; in this case, a key may need to be

---

[86] SP 800-38F, *Recommendation for Block Cipher Modes of Operation: Methods for Key Wrapping.*

[87] Note that this publication considers a passphrase or a PIN to be a password.

wrapped (i.e., encrypted and its integrity protected) or split into key components so that no single person can determine the key. These issues need to be addressed for operational keys.

Certain keys may need to be backed up so that if an operational key is inadvertently lost or modified, it can be recovered and operations resumed. Some keys may also need to be archived for long-term storage (e.g., because of legal requirements or to decrypt archived data). A key-recovery capability is needed whenever keys are backed up or archived. This capability needs to be designed so that the keys can be recovered in an acceptable amount of time and only by those entities authorized to do so; see SP 800-57, Part 1 for more information about key backup, key archiving, and the recovery of backed up and archived keys.

5.4.4 Cryptoperiods

A cryptoperiod is the time span during which a specific key is authorized for use. A cryptoperiod for a key is assigned for a number of reasons, including limiting the amount of exposure of encrypted data if a key is compromised. Cryptoperiods are usually assigned for a carefully considered period of time or by the maximum amount of data to be protected by the key. Tradeoffs associated with the determination of a cryptoperiod involve the risks and consequences of exposure. Section 5.3 of SP 800-57, Part 1 provides a more detailed discussion of the need for establishing cryptoperiods, the factors to be considered when deciding on a suitable cryptoperiod, and some suggestions for the length of cryptoperiods.

5.4.5 Use Validated Algorithms and Cryptographic Modules

Cryptographic algorithms must be validated and implemented in FIPS 140-validated cryptographic modules. Most IT products with cryptographic capabilities make claims as to the functionality and/or offered security of their product. When protecting sensitive data, the use of a FIPS 140-validated cryptographic module in those products provides a minimum level of assurance that the product's stated security claim is valid.

Federal agencies, private industry, and the public rely on cryptography for the protection of information and communications used in electronic commerce, the critical infrastructure, and other application areas. At the core of all products offering cryptographic services is the cryptographic module. Cryptographic modules, which contain cryptographic algorithms, are used in products and systems to provide security services such as confidentiality, integrity, and authentication. Although cryptography is used to provide security, weaknesses such as poor design or weak algorithms can render the product insecure and place highly sensitive information at risk. Adequate testing and validation of the cryptographic module and its underlying cryptographic algorithms against established standards is essential to providing security assurance.

NIST has established programs to validate the implementation of the **approved** cryptographic algorithms and the cryptographic modules in which they are used: the

Cryptographic Algorithm Validation Program (CAVP)[88] and the Cryptographic Module Validation Program (CMVP).[89]

See Section 5.1.2 in this document for a discussion of the security requirements for cryptographic modules.

5.4.6 Control of Keying Material

Access to keys needs to be controlled. A key **should** only be accessible by an authorized entity and only for the purpose for which it is authorized. For example, a key designated for key transport must not be used for the generation or verification of digital signatures.

The proliferation of keys also needs to be controlled. While it is often convenient to make copies of keys, these extra copies need to be accounted for. If a key is compromised, that key and all of its copies may need to be destroyed to prevent subsequent unauthorized use. For example, if a private key used for the generation of a digital signature is compromised, and a copy of the key still exists after the original copy was destroyed, then there is a possibility that the copy could be used to generate unauthorized digital signatures at a later time.

Users must be provided with a list of responsibilities and liabilities, and each user **should** sign a statement acknowledging these concerns before receiving a key. Users must be made aware of their unique responsibilities, especially regarding the significance of a key compromise or loss. Users must be able to store their secret and private keys securely so that no intruder can access them, yet the keys must be readily accessible for legitimate use.

5.4.7 Compromises

It is imperative to have a plan for handling the compromise or suspected compromise of keys, particularly those used and managed at a central site (e.g., the keys used by a CA to sign certificates). A compromise-recovery plan **should** be established before the system becomes operational and **should** address what actions will be taken with compromised system software and hardware, CA keys, user keys, previously generated signatures, encrypted data, etc. SP 800-57, Part 1 includes discussions of the effects of a key compromise, measures for minimizing the likelihood or consequences of a key compromise, and what **should** be considered in developing a compromise-recovery plan.

If someone's private or secret key is lost or compromised, other users must be made aware of this so that they will no longer initiate the protection of data using a compromised key or accept data protected with a compromised key without assessing and accepting the risk of doing so. This notification is often accomplished using CRLs or Compromised Key Lists (CKLs); see SP 800-57, Part 1 for discussions.

In some cases, a key and all copies of the key **should** be destroyed immediately upon the detection of a key compromise. For example, a private key used for the generation of digital signatures **should** be immediately destroyed. However, the corresponding public key may need to remain available for verifying the signatures that were previously generated using

---

[88] Information about the CAVP is available at https://csrc.nist.gov/projects/cavp.

[89] Information about the CMVP is available at https://csrc.nist.gov/projects/cmvp.

the compromised private key. Note that there is a risk associated with accepting these signatures.

5.4.8 Accountability and Inventory Management

Accountability involves the identification of those entities that have access to or control of cryptographic keys or certificates throughout their lifecycles. Accountability can be an effective tool to help prevent key compromises, reduce the impact of compromises when they are detected, determine the individuals that could have been involved when a compromise occurs, discourage key compromise because users know their access to the key is known, and determine where the key was used and what data or other keys were protected by a compromised key and, therefore, may also be compromised. When public key certificates are used, accountability is used to determine who is responsible for certificate maintenance (e.g., certificate replacement when a certificate expires or a private key is compromised).

The use of a key or certificate inventory can be a tool for assisting with accountability. Inventory management is concerned with establishing and maintaining an inventory of keys and/or certificates; assigning and tracking their owners, representatives, or sponsors (e.g., who or what they are, where they are located, and how to contact them); automating the entry of keys and certificates into the inventory; monitoring key and certificate status (e.g., expiration dates and whether a key has been compromised); and reporting the status to the appropriate official for remedial action, when required. SP 800-57, Part 1 provides discussions on both key and certificate inventory management.

5.4.9 Auditing

Auditing is a mechanism used for the prevention, detection, and recovery from key compromises. Several types of auditing need to be performed to assure proper key management:

- A compliance audit is a comprehensive review of an organization's adherence to regulatory guidelines. Compliance auditors review security policies (e.g., key management policies), as well as user access controls and risk-management procedures, to determine that these controls and procedures support the policies.

- An audit of the protective mechanisms employed (e.g., the cryptographic algorithms and key lengths used) is needed to reassess the level of security currently provided and expected to be required and provided in the future. This is needed to determine that the mechanisms correctly and effectively support the appropriate policies (e.g., the key management policies). New technology developments and attacks need to be taken into consideration.

- An audit of the actions of the humans that use, operate, and maintain the key management system is needed to verify that the humans continue to follow established security procedures. Highly unusual events are noted and reviewed as possible indicators of attempted attacks on the system.

6   Other Issues

The use of cryptography **should not** be undertaken without a thorough risk analysis and a determination of the sensitivity of the information to be protected and the security controls to be used (see FIPS 199, SP 800-175A, and SP 800-53). After performing a risk assessment and determining the sensitivity level of the information to be protected (Low, Moderate or High) and the security controls to be used, a number of issues need to be addressed to ensure that cryptography is used properly.

This section identifies issues to be addressed after determining that cryptography is required for an application.

6.1   Required Security Strength

The minimum security strength is determined by the sensitivity level of the information (see FIPS 199). SP 800-152 requires a security strength of at least 112 bits for the protection of Low-impact information, 128 bits for Moderate-impact information, and 192 bits for High-impact information. The required security strength can then be used to determine the algorithm and key size to be used. Section 5.6 of SP 800-57, Part 1 provides tables for selecting appropriate algorithms and key sizes.

Many applications require the use of several different cryptographic algorithms. Ideally, these algorithms would all offer the same security strength, but this may not always be the case for performance, availability, and interoperability reasons. When algorithms of different strengths are used together to protect data, the security provided by the combination of algorithms is the strength associated with the algorithm with the lowest security strength (see Section 5.6 of SP 800-57, Part 1). For example, RSA with 2048-bit keys can support a security strength of 112 bits but is often used with SHA-256, which can support a security strength of 128 bits. When the combination is used to generate a digital signature, the signature can only provide a security strength of 112 bits – the lesser strength offered by the two algorithms.

Approved combinations of algorithms (called cipher suites) for some of the protocols are provided in SP 800-57, Part 3 (for S/MIME) and SP 800-52 (for TLS).

6.2   Interoperability

Interoperability is the ability of one entity to communicate with another entity, whether the entities are people, devices, or processes. In order to communicate, the entities must have

1. A communications channel (e.g., the Internet) and the same communications protocol (e.g., TLS), and

2. Policies that allow the entities to communicate.

In order to communicate securely, the entities must also

3. Have trust that each entity will enforce its own policies,

4. Have interoperable cryptographic capabilities as discussed in Section 4, and

5. Share appropriate keying material that has been established securely (see Section 5.3).

For example, if entities A and B are in two different organizations, and

- Each organization has a policy that allows the entities to communicate,

- Each entity trusts that the other entity will enforce its own policies,

- There is a TLS capability that can be used for communication,

- Each entity can encrypt and decrypt information using AES with a 128-bit key and establish keys using 3072-bit RSA key transport (see Section 5.3.4.1), and

- One of the entities can generate a 128-bit AES key and act as the sender in the key-transport scheme, and the other entity has a 3072-bit RSA key pair and can act as the receiver,

then the two entities have a secure and interoperable communication channel that can be used to establish a 128-bit key for encrypting information using AES. In this case, the security strength that can be provided by an encryption operation using AES is 128 bits, since both 3072-bit RSA and AES-128 are rated at a security strength of 128 bits (see Section 6.1).

6.3   When Algorithms are No Longer Approved

In the case that an algorithm is **no longer approved** for providing adequate protection (e.g., the algorithm may have been "broken"), a risk assessment needs to be performed to determine whether the information should be re-protected using an **approved** algorithm and key size that will protect the information for the remainder of its security life. See Section 5.6.4 of SP 800-57, Part 1 for additional discussion.

References

NIST Publications

The following FIPS and NIST Special Publications (SP) apply to the use of cryptography in the Federal Government.

FIPS 140   National Institute of Standards and Technology (2019) Security Requirements for Cryptographic Modules. (U.S. Department of Commerce, Washington, D.C.), Federal Information Processing Standards Publication (FIPS) 140-3.
https://doi.org/10.6028/NIST.FIPS.140-3

> *FIPS 140-3 specifies the requirements that must be met by cryptographic modules protecting U.S. Government information. The standard provides four increasing, qualitative levels of security. The security requirements cover areas related to the secure design and implementation of a cryptographic module.*

FIPS 180   National Institute of Standards and Technology (2015) Secure Hash Standard (SHS). (U.S. Department of Commerce, Washington, D.C.), Federal Information Processing Standards Publication (FIPS) 180-4.
https://doi.org/10.6028/NIST.FIPS.180-4

> *FIPS 180-4 specifies seven cryptographic hash algorithms: SHA-1, SHA-224, SHA-256, SHA-384, SHA-512, SHA-512/224, and SHA-512/256.*

FIPS 185   National Institute of Standards and Technology (1994), Escrowed Encryption Standard, (U.S. Department of Commerce, Washington, D.C.), Federal Information Processing Standards Publication (FIPS) 185. Withdrawn October 19, 2015.
https://csrc.nist.gov/CSRC/media/Publications/fips/185/archive/1994-02-09/documents/fips185.pdf

> *FIPS 185 specified the use of an encryption/decryption algorithm and a Law Enforcement Access Field (LEAF) creation method that could be implemented in electronic devices and used for protecting government telecommunications when such protection was desired. The algorithm and the LEAF creation method were classified. The LEAF was intended for use in a key-escrow system that provided for the decryption of telecommunications when access to the telecommunications was lawfully authorized.*

FIPS 186   National Institute of Standards and Technology (2013) Digital Signature Standard (DSS). (U.S. Department of Commerce, Washington, D.C.), Federal Information Processing Standards Publication (FIPS) 186-4.

https://doi.org/10.6028/NIST.FIPS.186-4

National Institute of Standards and Technology (2019 Draft) Digital Signature Standard (DSS). (U.S. Department of Commerce, Washington, D.C.), Federal Information Processing Standards Publication (FIPS) 186-5.
https://doi.org/10.6028/NIST.FIPS.186-5-draft

> *FIPS 186 specifies a suite of algorithms that can be used to generate a digital signature. Digital signatures are used to detect unauthorized modifications to data and to authenticate the identity of the signatory. In addition, the recipient of signed data can use a digital signature as evidence in demonstrating to a third party that the signature was, in fact, generated by the claimed signatory. This is known as non-repudiation since the signatory cannot easily repudiate the signature at a later time.*

FIPS 197   National Institute of Standards and Technology (2001) Advanced Encryption Standard (AES). (U.S. Department of Commerce, Washington, D.C.), Federal Information Processing Standards Publication (FIPS) 197.
https://doi.org/10.6028/NIST.FIPS.197

> *FIPS 197 specifies a symmetric-key block cipher algorithm. The Standard supports key sizes of 128, 192, and 256 bits and a block size of 128 bits.*

FIPS 198   National Institute of Standards and Technology (2008) The Keyed-Hash Message Authentication Code (HMAC). (U.S. Department of Commerce, Washington, D.C.), Federal Information Processing Standards Publication (FIPS) 198-1.
https://doi.org/10.6028/NIST.FIPS.198-1

> *FIPS 198-1 defines a message authentication code (MAC) that uses a cryptographic hash function in conjunction with a secret key for the calculation and verification of the MAC.*

FIPS 199   National Institute of Standards and Technology (2004) Standards for Security Categorization of Federal Information and Information Systems. (U.S. Department of Commerce, Washington, D.C.), Federal Information Processing Standards Publication (FIPS) 199.
https://doi.org/10.6028/NIST.FIPS.199

> *FIPS 199 establishes security categories for both information and information systems. The security categories are based on the potential impact on an organization if certain events occur that jeopardize the information and information systems needed by the organization to accomplish its assigned mission, protect its assets,*

*fulfill its legal responsibilities, maintain its day-to-day functions,
and protect individuals.*

FIPS 202   National Institute of Standards and Technology (2015) SHA-3
Standard: Permutation-Based Hash and Extendable-Output
Functions. (U.S. Department of Commerce, Washington, D.C.),
Federal Information Processing Standards Publication (FIPS) 202.
https://doi.org/10.6028/NIST.FIPS.202

> *FIPS 202 specifies SHA3-224, SHA3-256, SHA3-384, and SHA3-512. This FIPS also specifies two extendable-output functions (SHAKE128 and SHAKE256), which are not, in themselves, considered to be hash functions.*

SP 800-21   Barker EB, Barker WC, Lee A (2005) Guideline for Implementing
Cryptography in the Federal Government. (National Institute of
Standards and Technology, Gaithersburg, MD), NIST Special
Publication (SP) 800-21 2nd edition. Withdrawn August 27, 2016.
https://doi.org/10.6028/NIST.SP.800-21e2

> *NIST SP 800-21 provides a structured, yet flexible set of
> guidelines for selecting, specifying, employing, and evaluating
> cryptographic protection mechanisms in Federal information
> systems.*

SP 800-22   Bassham LE III, Rukhin A, Soto J, Nechvatal JR, Smid ME, Barker
EB, Leigh SD, Levenson M, Vangel M, Banks D, Heckert NA, Dray
JF, Jr. (2010) A Statistical Test Suite for Random and Pseudorandom
Number Generators for Cryptographic Applications. (National
Institute of Standards and Technology, Gaithersburg, MD), NIST
Special Publication (SP) 800-22, Rev. 1a.
https://doi.org/10.6028/NIST.SP.800-22r1a

> *SP 800-22 discusses some aspects of selecting and testing random
> and pseudorandom number generators for providing random
> numbers that are indistinguishable from truly random output.*

SP 800-32   Kuhn R, Hu VC, Polk T, Chang S-jH (2001) Introduction to Public
Key Technology and the Federal PKI Infrastructure. (National
Institute of Standards and Technology, Gaithersburg, MD), NIST
Special Publication (SP) 800-32.
https://doi.org/10.6028/NIST.SP.800-32

> *SP 800-32 was developed to assist agency decision-makers in
> determining if a PKI is appropriate for their agency and how PKI
> services can be deployed most effectively within a federal agency.
> It is intended to provide an overview of PKI functions and their
> applications.*

SP 800-38   A series of publications specifying modes of operation for block cipher algorithms (see below).

SP 800-38A   Dworkin MJ (2001) Recommendation for Block Cipher Modes of Operation: Methods and Techniques. (National Institute of Standards and Technology, Gaithersburg, MD), NIST Special Publication (SP) 800-38A.
https://doi.org/10.6028/NIST.SP.800-38A

SP 800-38A defines five confidentiality modes of operation for use with an underlying symmetric-key block cipher algorithm: Electronic Codebook (ECB), Cipher Block Chaining (CBC), Cipher Feedback (CFB), Output Feedback (OFB), and Counter (CTR). When used with an **approved** *underlying block cipher algorithm (i.e., AES or TDEA), these modes can provide cryptographic protection for sensitive computer data.*

SP 800-38B   Dworkin MJ (2005) Recommendation for Block Cipher Modes of Operation: the CMAC Mode for Authentication. (National Institute of Standards and Technology, Gaithersburg, MD), NIST Special Publication (SP) 800-38B, Includes updates as of October 6, 2016.
https://doi.org/10.6028/NIST.SP.800-38B

SP 800-38B specifies a message authentication code (MAC) algorithm based on a symmetric-key block cipher (i.e., AES or TDEA). This block cipher-based MAC algorithm, called CMAC, may be used to provide assurance of the source and integrity of binary data.

SP 800-38C   Dworkin MJ (2004) Recommendation for Block Cipher Modes of Operation: the CCM Mode for Authentication and Confidentiality. (National Institute of Standards and Technology, Gaithersburg, MD), NIST Special Publication (SP) 800-38C, Includes updates as of July 20, 2007.
https://doi.org/10.6028/NIST.SP.800-38C

SP 800-38C defines a mode of operation, called CCM, for a symmetric-key block cipher algorithm with a 128-bit block size (i.e., AES). CCM may be used to provide assurance of the confidentiality and authenticity of computer data by combining the techniques of the Counter (CTR) mode specified in SP 800-38A with the Cipher Block Chaining-Message Authentication Code (CBC-MAC) algorithm (specified in SP 800-90B but **not** *currently approved for general use).*

SP 800-38D   Dworkin MJ (2007) Recommendation for Block Cipher Modes of Operation: Galois/Counter Mode (GCM) and GMAC. (National

Institute of Standards and Technology, Gaithersburg, MD), NIST
Special Publication (SP) 800-38D.
https://doi.org/10.6028/NIST.SP.800-38D

*SP 800-38D specifies the Galois/Counter Mode (GCM), an
algorithm for authenticated encryption with associated data, and
its specialization, GMAC, for generating a message authentication
code (MAC) on data that is not encrypted. GCM and GMAC are
modes of operation for an underlying,* **approved** *symmetric-key
block cipher with a 128-bit block size (i.e., AES).*

SP 800-38E   Dworkin MJ (2010) Recommendation for Block Cipher Modes of
Operation: the XTS-AES Mode for Confidentiality on Storage
Devices. (National Institute of Standards and Technology,
Gaithersburg, MD), NIST Special Publication (SP) 800-38E.
https://doi.org/10.6028/NIST.SP.800-38E

*SP 800-38E approves the XTS-AES mode of the AES algorithm by
reference to IEEE 1619, with one additional requirement, as an
option for protecting the confidentiality of data on storage devices.
The mode does not provide authentication of the data or its source.*

SP 800-38F   Dworkin MJ (2012) Recommendation for Block Cipher Modes of
Operation: Methods for Key Wrapping. (National Institute of
Standards and Technology, Gaithersburg, MD), NIST Special
Publication (SP) 800-38F.
https://doi.org/10.6028/NIST.SP.800-38F

*SP 800-38F describes cryptographic methods that are approved
for key wrapping. In addition to approving existing methods, this
publication specifies two new, deterministic authenticated-
encryption modes of operation of the Advanced Encryption
Standard (AES) algorithm: the AES Key Wrap (KW) mode and the
AES Key Wrap with Padding (KWP) mode. An analogous mode
with the Triple Data Encryption Algorithm (TDEA) as the
underlying block cipher, called TKW, is also specified to support
legacy applications.*

SP 800-38G   Dworkin MJ (2019) Recommendation for Block Cipher Modes of
Operation: Methods for Format-Preserving Encryption. (National
Institute of Standards and Technology, Gaithersburg, MD), Draft
NIST Special Publication (SP) 800-38G Revision 1.
https://doi.org/10.6028/NIST.SP.800-38Gr1-draft

*SP 800-38G specifies two methods, called FF1 and FF3, for
format-preserving encryption. Both of these methods are modes of
operation for an underlying,* **approved** *symmetric-key block cipher
algorithm.*

SP 800-52   McKay KA, Cooper DA (2019) Guidelines for the Selection,
                 Configuration, and Use of Transport Layer Security (TLS)
                 Implementations. (National Institute of Standards and Technology,
                 Gaithersburg, MD), NIST Special Publication (SP) 800-52, Rev. 2.
                 https://doi.org/10.6028/NIST.SP.800-52r2

                 *Transport Layer Security (TLS) provides mechanisms to protect
                 data during electronic dissemination across the Internet. SP 800-
                 52 provides guidance to the selection and configuration of TLS
                 protocol implementations while making effective use of FIPS and
                 NIST-recommended cryptographic algorithms. It requires that TLS
                 1.2 configured with FIPS-based cipher suites be supported by all
                 government TLS servers and clients and requires support for TLS
                 1.3 by January 1, 2024. This publication also provides guidance
                 on certificates and TLS extensions that impact security.*

SP 800-53   Joint Task Force Transformation Initiative (2017) Security and
                 Privacy Controls for Information Systems and Organizations.
                 (National Institute of Standards and Technology, Gaithersburg, MD),
                 Draft NIST Special Publication (SP) 800-53, Rev. 5.
                 https://csrc.nist.gov/publications/detail/sp/800-53/rev-5/draft

                 *SP 800-53 provides a catalog of security and privacy controls for
                 federal information systems and organizations and a process for
                 selecting controls to protect organizational operations (including
                 mission, functions, image, and reputation), organizational assets,
                 individuals, other organizations, and the Nation from a diverse set
                 of threats, including hostile cyber attacks, natural disasters,
                 structural failures, and human errors.*

SP 800-56A   Barker EB, Chen L, Roginsky A, Vassilev A, Davis R (2018)
                 Recommendation for Pair-Wise Key-Establishment Schemes Using
                 Discrete Logarithm Cryptography. (National Institute of Standards
                 and Technology, Gaithersburg, MD), NIST Special Publication (SP)
                 800-56A, Rev. 3.
                 https://doi.org/10.6028/NIST.SP.800-56Ar3

                 *SP 800-56A specifies key-establishment schemes based on the
                 discrete logarithm problem over finite fields and elliptic curves,
                 including several variations of Diffie–Hellman and
                 Menezes–Qu–Vanstone (MQV) key-establishment schemes.*

SP 800-56B   Barker EB, Chen L, Roginsky A, Vassilev A, Davis R, Simon S
                 (2019) Recommendation for Pair-Wise Key-Establishment Using
                 Integer Factorization Cryptography. (National Institute of Standards
                 and Technology, Gaithersburg, MD), NIST Special Publication (SP)
                 800-56B, Rev. 2.

67

https://doi.org/10.6028/NIST.SP.800-56Br2

SP 800-56B specifies key-establishment schemes using integer-factorization cryptography (RSA). Both key transport and key-agreement schemes are specified.

SP 800-56C   Barker EB, Chen L, Davis R (2018) Recommendation for Key-Derivation Methods in Key-Establishment Schemes. (National Institute of Standards and Technology, Gaithersburg, MD), NIST Special Publication (SP) 800-56C, Rev. 1.
https://doi.org/10.6028/NIST.SP.800-56Cr1

SP 800-56C specifies techniques for the derivation of keying material from a shared secret established during a key-establishment scheme defined in SP 800-56A or SP 800-56B.

SP 800-57,   Barker EB (2019) Recommendation for Key Management: Part 1 –
Part 1   General. (National Institute of Standards and Technology, Gaithersburg, MD), Draft NIST Special Publication (SP) 800-57 Part 1, Rev. 5.
https://doi.org/10.6028/NIST.SP.800-57pt1r5-draft

Part 1 of SP 800-57 provides general guidance and best practices for the management of cryptographic keying material, including definitions of the security services that may be provided when using cryptographyand the algorithms and key types that may be employed,specifications ofthe protection that each type of key and other cryptographic informationrequires and methods for providing this protection,discussions about thefunctions involved in key management,and discussions abouta variety of key-management issues to be addressed when using cryptography.

SP 800-57,   Barker EB, Barker WC (2019) Recommendation for Key
Part 2   Management: Part 2 – Best Practices for Key Management Organizations. (National Institute of Standards and Technology, Gaithersburg, MD), NIST Special Publication (SP) 800-57 Part 2, Rev. 1.
https://doi.org/10.6028/NIST.SP.800-57pt2r1

Part 2 of SP 800-57 provides guidance on policy and security planning requirements for U.S. government agencies. This part of SP 800-57 contains a generic key-management infrastructure, guidance for the development of organizational key-management policy statements and key-management practices statements, an identification of key-management information that needs to be incorporated into security plans for general support systems and major applications that employ cryptography, and an

*identification of key-management information that needs to be
documented for all federal applications of cryptography.*

SP 800-57, Part 3	Barker EB, Dang QH (2015) Recommendation for Key Management, Part 3: Application-Specific Key Management Guidance. (National Institute of Standards and Technology, Gaithersburg, MD), NIST Special Publication (SP) 800-57 Part 3, Rev. 1. https://doi.org/10.6028/NIST.SP.800-57pt3r1

*Part 3 of SP 800-57 addresses the key-management issues
associated with currently available cryptographic mechanisms,
such as the Public Key Infrastructure (PKI), Internet Protocol
Security (IPsec), Secure/Multipart Internet Mail Extensions
(S/MIME), Kerberos, Over-the-Air Rekeying (OTAR), Domain
Name System Security Extensions (DNSSEC), Encrypted File
Systems, and the Secure Shell (SSH) protocol.*

SP 800-67	Barker EB, Mouha N (2017) Recommendation for the Triple Data Encryption Algorithm (TDEA) Block Cipher. (National Institute of Standards and Technology, Gaithersburg, MD), NIST Special Publication (SP) 800-67, Rev. 2. https://doi.org/10.6028/NIST.SP.800-67r2

*SP 800-67 specifies the Triple Data Encryption Algorithm (TDEA),
including its primary component cryptographic engine, the Data
Encryption Algorithm (DEA).*

SP 800-71	Barker EB, Barker WC (2018), Recommendation for Key Establishment Using Symmetric Block Ciphers. (National Institute of Standards and Technology, Gaithersburg, MD), Draft NIST Special Publication (SP) 800-71. https://csrc.nist.gov/publications/detail/sp/800-71/draft

*SP 800-71 addresses the protection of symmetric keying material
during a key establishment that uses symmetric-key cryptography
for key distribution. The Recommendation also addresses recovery
in the event of detectable errors during the key-distribution process.
Wrapping mechanisms are specified for encrypting keys, binding
key control information to the keys, and protecting the integrity of
this information.*

SP 800-89	Barker EB (2006) Recommendation for Obtaining Assurances for Digital Signature Applications. (National Institute of Standards and Technology, Gaithersburg, MD), NIST Special Publication (SP) 800-89. https://doi.org/10.6028/NIST.SP.800-89

*Entities participating in the generation or verification of digital
signatures depend on the authenticity of the process. SP 800-89*

specifies methods for obtaining the assurances necessary for valid digital signatures: assurance of domain parameter validity, assurance of public key validity, assurance that the key-pair owner actually possesses the private key, and assurance of the identity of the key-pair owner.

SP 800-90A   Barker EB, Kelsey JM (2015) Recommendation for Random Number Generation Using Deterministic Random Bit Generators. (National Institute of Standards and Technology, Gaithersburg, MD), NIST Special Publication (SP) 800-90A, Rev. 1.
https://doi.org/10.6028/NIST.SP.800-90Ar1

SP 800-90A specifies DRBG mechanisms for the generation of random bits using deterministic methods. The methods provided are based on either hash functions or block cipher algorithms and are designed to support selected security strengths. DRBGs must be initialized from a randomness source that provides sufficient entropy for the security strength to be supported by the DRBG.

SP 800-90B   Sönmez Turan M, Barker EB, Kelsey JM, McKay KA, Baish ML, Boyle M (2018) Recommendation for the Entropy Sources Used for Random Bit Generation. (National Institute of Standards and Technology, Gaithersburg, MD), NIST Special Publication (SP) 800-90B.
https://doi.org/10.6028/NIST.SP.800-90B

SP 800-90B specifies the design principles and requirements for the entropy sources used by Random Bit Generators, including health tests to determine that the entropy source has not failed and tests for the validation of entropy sources.

SP 800-90C   Barker EB, Kelsey JM (2016), Recommendation for Random Bit Generator (RBG) Constructions. (National Institute of Standards and Technology, Gaithersburg, MD), Draft NIST Special Publication (SP) 800-90C.
https://csrc.nist.gov/publications/detail/sp/800-90c/draft

SP 800-90C specifies constructions for the implementation of random bit generators (RBGs). An RBG may be a deterministic random bit generator (DRBG) or a non-deterministic random bit generator (NRBG). The constructed RBGs consist of DRBG mechanisms as specified SP 800-90A and entropy sources as specified in SP 800-90B.

SP 800-102   Barker EB (2009) Recommendation for Digital Signature Timeliness. (National Institute of Standards and Technology, Gaithersburg, MD), NIST Special Publication (SP) 800-102.
https://doi.org/10.6028/NIST.SP.800-102

Establishing the time when a digital signature was generated is often a critical consideration. A signed message that includes the (purported) signing time provides no assurance that the private key was used to sign the message at that time unless the accuracy of the time can be trusted. With the appropriate use of digital signature-based timestamps from a Trusted Timestamp Authority and/or verifier-supplied data that is included in the signed message, the signer can provide some level of assurance about the time that the message was signed.

SP 800-106   Dang QH (2009) Randomized Hashing for Digital Signatures. (National Institute of Standards and Technology, Gaithersburg, MD), NIST Special Publication (SP) 800-106.
https://doi.org/10.6028/NIST.SP.800-106

*NIST-approved digital signature algorithms require the use of an **approved** cryptographic hash function during the generation and verification of signatures. SP 800-106 specifies a method to enhance the security of the cryptographic hash functions used in digital signature applications by randomizing the messages that are signed.*

SP 800-107   Dang QH (2012) Recommendation for Applications Using Approved Hash Algorithms. (National Institute of Standards and Technology, Gaithersburg, MD), NIST Special Publication (SP) 800-107, Rev. 1.
https://doi.org/10.6028/NIST.SP.800-107r1

*Hash functions that compute a fixed-length message digest from arbitrary-length messages are widely used for many purposes in information security. SP 800-107 provides security guidelines for achieving the required or desired security strengths for cryptographic applications that employ the **approved** hash functions specified in FIPS 180. These include the generation and verification of digital signatures and Keyed-hash Message Authentication Codes (HMACs) and the use of Hashed-based Key Derivation Functions (hash-based KDFs).*

SP 800-108   Chen L (2009) Recommendation for Key Derivation Using Pseudorandom Functions (Revised). (National Institute of Standards and Technology, Gaithersburg, MD), NIST Special Publication (SP) 800-108, Revised.
https://doi.org/10.6028/NIST.SP.800-108

SP 800-108 specifies techniques for the derivation of additional keying material from a pre-shared secret key (i.e., a key-derivation key) using pseudorandom functions. The key-derivation key may have either been established through a key-establishment scheme or shared through some other manner (e.g., a manual key distribution).

SP 800-130　　　Barker EB, Smid ME, Branstad DK, Chokhani S (2013) A Framework for Designing Cryptographic Key Management Systems. (National Institute of Standards and Technology, Gaithersburg, MD), NIST Special Publication (SP) 800-130.
https://doi.org/10.6028/NIST.SP.800-130

　　　　　　　　SP 800-130 contains topics to be considered by a CKMS designer when developing a CKMS design specification. Topics include security policies, cryptographic keys and metadata, interoperability and transitioning, security controls, testing and system assurances, disaster recovery, and security assessments.

SP 800-131A　　Barker EB, Roginsky A (2019) Transitioning the Use of Cryptographic Algorithms and Key Lengths. (National Institute of Standards and Technology, Gaithersburg, MD), NIST Special Publication (SP) 800-131A, Rev. 2.
https://doi.org/10.6028/NIST.SP.800-131Ar2

　　　　　　　　Section 5.6.4 of SP 800-57, Part 1 provides recommendations for transitioning to new cryptographic algorithms and key lengths because of algorithm breaks or the availability of more powerful computers that could be used to efficiently search for cryptographic keys. SP 800-131A offers more specific guidance for such transitions. Each algorithm and service is addressed in SP 800-131A, indicating whether its use is acceptable, deprecated, restricted, allowed only for legacy applications[90], or disallowed.

SP 800-132　　　Sönmez Turan M, Barker EB, Burr WE, Chen L (2010) Recommendation for Password-Based Key Derivation: Part 1: Storage Applications. (National Institute of Standards and Technology, Gaithersburg, MD), NIST Special Publication (SP) 800-132.
https://doi.org/10.6028/NIST.SP.800-132

　　　　　　　　SP 800-132 specifies techniques for the derivation of master keys from passwords or passphrases to protect stored electronic data or data protection keys.

SP 800-133　　　Barker EB, Roginsky A (2019) Recommendation for Cryptographic Key Generation. (National Institute of Standards and Technology, Gaithersburg, MD), NIST Special Publication (SP) 800-133 Revision 1.

---

[90] The algorithm and key length may be used to process already-protected information, but there may be a risk in doing so.

https://doi.org/10.6028/NIST.SP.800-133r1

SP 800-133 discusses the generation of the keys to be managed and used by the **approved** *cryptographic algorithms.*

SP 800-135   Dang QH (2011) Recommendation for Existing Application-Specific Key Derivation Functions. (National Institute of Standards and Technology, Gaithersburg, MD), NIST Special Publication (SP) 800-135, Rev. 1.
https://doi.org/10.6028/NIST.SP.800-135r1

Many widely-used internet security protocols have their own application-specific Key Derivation Functions (KDFs) that are used to generate the cryptographic keys required for their cryptographic functions. SP 800-135 provides security requirements for those KDFs.

SP 800-152   Barker EB, Branstad DK, Smid ME (2015) A Profile for U.S. Federal Cryptographic Key Management Systems (CKMS). (National Institute of Standards and Technology, Gaithersburg, MD), NIST Special Publication (SP) 800-152.
https://doi.org/10.6028/NIST.SP.800-152

SP 800-152 contains requirements for the design, implementation, procurement, installation, configuration, management, operation, and use of a CKMS by and for U.S. federal organizations and their contractors. The Profile is based on SP 800-130.

SP 800-175A   Barker EB, Barker WC (2016) Guideline for Using Cryptographic Standards in the Federal Government: Directives, Mandates, and Policies. (National Institute of Standards and Technology, Gaithersburg, MD), NIST Special Publication (SP) 800-175A.
https://doi.org/10.6028/NIST.SP.800-175A

SP 800-175A provides guidance on the determination of requirements for using cryptography. It includes a summary of laws and regulations concerning the protection of the Federal Government's sensitive information, guidance regarding the conduct of risk assessments to determine what needs to be protected and how best to protect that information, and a discussion of the relevant security-related documents (e.g., various policy and practice documents).

SP 800-185   Kelsey JM, Chang S-j, Perlner RA (2016) SHA-3 Derived Functions: cSHAKE, KMAC, TupleHash, and ParallelHash. (National Institute of Standards and Technology, Gaithersburg, MD), NIST Special Publication (SP) 800-185.
https://doi.org/10.6028/NIST.SP.800-185

This Recommendation specifies four types of SHA-3-derived functions: cSHAKE, KMAC, TupleHash, and ParallelHash, each defined for a 128- and 256-bit security strength. cSHAKE is a customizable variant of the SHAKE function, as defined in FIPS 202. KMAC (for KECCAK Message Authentication Code) is a variable-length message authentication code algorithm based on KECCAK; it can also be used as a pseudorandom function. TupleHash is a variable-length hash function designed to hash tuples of input strings without trivial collisions. ParallelHash is a variable-length hash function that can hash very long messages in parallel.

SP 800-186   Chen L, Moody D, Regenscheid A (2019) Recommendation for Discrete-Logarithm Based Cryptography: Elliptic Curve Domain Parameters. (National Institute of Standards and Technology, Gaithersburg, MD), Draft NIST Special Publication (SP) 800-186. https://doi.org/10.6028/NIST.SP.800-186-draft

SP 800-186 specifies the set of elliptic curves recommended for U.S. Government use. In addition to the previously recommended Weierstrass curves defined over prime fields and binary fields, this recommendation includes two newly specified Montgomery curves, which claim increased performance, side-channel resistance, and simpler implementation when compared to traditional curves. The recommendation also specifies alternative representations for these new curves to allow more implementation flexibility. The new curves are interoperable with those specified by the Crypto Forum Research Group (CFRG) of the Internet Engineering Task Force (IETF).

NISTIR 7924   Booth H, Regenscheid A (2014) Reference Certificate Policy. (National Institute of Standards and Technology, Gaithersburg, MD), Second Draft NIST Interagency or Internal Report (IR) 7924. Available at https://csrc.nist.gov/publications/detail/nistir/7924/draft

NISTIR 7924 is intended to identify a set of security controls and practices to support the secure issuance of certificates. It was written in the form of a Certificate Policy (CP), a standard format for defining the expectations and requirements of the relying party community that will trust the certificates issued by its Certificate Authorities (CAs).

NISTIR 7977   Cryptographic Technology Group (2016) NIST Cryptographic Standards and Guidelines Development Process. (National Institute of Standards and Technology, Gaithersburg, MD), NIST Interagency or Internal Report (IR) 7977.

74

https://doi.org/10.6028/NIST.IR.7977

*NISTIR 7977 describes the principles, processes and procedures
that drive cryptographic standards and guidelines development
efforts at NIST.*

Non-NIST Publications

IEEE 802.11	Institute of Electrical and Electronics Engineers (2016) *IEEE 802.11-2016 – IEEE Standard for Information technology-- Telecommunications and information exchange between systems Local and metropolitan area networks--Specific requirements - Part 11: Wireless LAN Medium Access Control (MAC) and Physical Layer (PHY) Specifications* (IEEE, Piscataway, NJ). Available at https://standards.ieee.org/content/ieee-standards/en/standard/802_11-2016.html
IEEE 1363	Institute of Electrical and Electronics Engineers (2000) *IEEE 1363-2000 – IEEE Standard Specifications for Public-Key Cryptography* (IEEE, Piscataway, NJ). Available at. Available at https://standards.ieee.org/standard/1363-2000.html
IEEE 1363a	Institute of Electrical and Electronics Engineers (2004) *IEEE 1363a-2004 – IEEE Standard Specifications for Public Key Cryptography – Amendment 1: Additional Techniques* (IEEE, Piscataway, NJ). Available at https://standards.ieee.org/standard/1363a-2004.html
IEEE 1363.1	Institute of Electrical and Electronics Engineers (2008) *IEEE 1363.1-2008 – IEEE Standard Specification for Public Key Cryptographic Techniques Based on Hard Problems over Lattices* (IEEE, Piscataway, NJ). Available at https://standards.ieee.org/standard/1363_1-2008.html
IEEE 1363.2	Institute of Electrical and Electronics Engineers (2008) *IEEE 1363.2-2008 – IEEE Standard Specification for Password-Based Public-Key Cryptography* (IEEE, Piscataway, NJ). Available at https://standards.ieee.org/standard/1363_2-2008.html
IEEE 1619	Institute of Electrical and Electronics Engineers, *Standard for Cryptographic Protection of Data on Block-Oriented Storage Devices*, IEEE 1619, (multiple parts), 2008 (IEEE, Piscataway, NJ). Available at https://standards.ieee.org/content/ieee-standards/en/standard/1619-2018.html

ISO/IEC 9594-8   International Organization for Standardization/International Electrotechnical Commission (2017) *ISO/IEC 9594-8:2017 – Information technology – Open Systems Interconnection – The Directory – Part 8: Public-key and attribute certificate frameworks* (ISO, Geneva, Switzerland). Available at https://www.iso.org/standard/72557.html

This specification is also published as International Telecommunications Union (2019) ITU-T X.509 (10/2019) – Information technology – Open Systems Interconnection – The Directory: Public-key and attribute certificate frameworks (ITU, Geneva, Switzerland). Available at https://www.itu.int/itu-t/recommendations/rec.aspx?rec=X.509.).

ISO/IEC 9797-1   International Organization for Standardization/International Electrotechnical Commission (2011) *ISO/IEC 9797-1:2011 – Information technology – Security techniques – Message Authentication Codes (MACs) – Part 1: Mechanisms using a block cipher* (ISO, Geneva, Switzerland). Available at https://www.iso.org/standard/50375.html

This standard includes CMAC, as specified in SP 800-38B.

ISO/IEC 9797-2   International Organization for Standardization/International Electrotechnical Commission (2011) *ISO/IEC 9797-2:2011 – Information technology – Security techniques – Message Authentication Codes (MACs) – Part 2: Mechanisms using a dedicated hash-function* (ISO, Geneva, Switzerland). Available at https://www.iso.org/standard/51618.html

This standard includes HMAC, as specified in FIPS 198.

ISO/IEC 10116   International Organization for Standardization/International Electrotechnical Commission (2017) *ISO/IEC 10116:2017 – Information technology – Security techniques – Modes of operation for an n-bit block cipher* (ISO, Geneva, Switzerland). Available at https://www.iso.org/standard/64575.html

This standard includes all the modes specified in SP 800-38A.

ISO/IEC 10118-3   International Organization for Standardization/International Electrotechnical Commission (2018) *ISO/IEC 10118-3:2018 – Information technology – Security techniques – Hash-functions – Part 3: Dedicated hash-functions* (ISO, Geneva, Switzerland). Available at https://www.iso.org/standard/67116.html

*This standard includes SHA-1 and the SHA-2 family of hash
functions specified in FIPS 180. A revision of ISO/IEC 10118-3 will
include the SHA-3 functions specified in FIPS 202.*

ISO/IEC 11770-3   International Organization for Standardization/International
Electrotechnical Commission (2015) *ISO/IEC 11770-3:2015 –
Information technology – Security techniques – Key management –
Part 3: Mechanisms using asymmetric techniques* (ISO, Geneva,
Switzerland). Available at
https://www.iso.org/standard/60237.html

*This standard specifies key establishment mechanisms, some of
which can be instantiated with key-establishment schemes specified
in SP 800-56A and SP 800-56B.*

ISO/IEC 11770-6   International Organization for Standardization/International
Electrotechnical Commission (2016) *ISO/IEC 11770-6:2016 –
Information technology – Security techniques – Key management –
Part 6: Key derivation* (ISO, Geneva, Switzerland). Available at
https://www.iso.org/standard/65275.html

*This draft standard will include all key derivation functions
specified in SP 800-108, as well as the two-step key derivation
method specified in SP 800-56C.*

ISO/IEC 11889   This multi-part standard includes:

International Organization for Standardization/International
Electrotechnical Commission (2015) *ISO/IEC 11889-1:2015 –
Information technology – Trusted Platform Module Library – Part 1:
Architecture* (ISO, Geneva, Switzerland). Available at
https://www.iso.org/standard/66510.html

International Organization for Standardization/International
Electrotechnical Commission (2015) *ISO/IEC 11889-2:2015 –
Information technology – Trusted Platform Module Library – Part 2:
Structures* (ISO, Geneva, Switzerland). Available at
https://www.iso.org/standard/66511.html

International Organization for Standardization/International
Electrotechnical Commission (2015) *ISO/IEC 11889-3:2015 –
Information technology – Trusted Platform Module Library – Part 3:
Commands* (ISO, Geneva, Switzerland). Available at
https://www.iso.org/standard/66512.html

International Organization for Standardization/International
Electrotechnical Commission (2015) *ISO/IEC 11889-4:2015 –
Information technology – Trusted Platform Module Library – Part 4:
Supporting Routines* (ISO, Geneva, Switzerland). Available at

https://www.iso.org/standard/66513.html

ISO/IEC 14888-2   International Organization for Standardization/International
Electrotechnical Commission (2008) *ISO/IEC 14888-2:2008 −
Information technology − Security techniques − Digital signatures
with appendix − Part 2: Integer factorization-based mechanisms* (ISO,
Geneva, Switzerland). Available at
https://www.iso.org/standard/44227.html

      This standard includes RSA signatures, as specified in FIPS 186.

ISO/IEC 14888-3   International Organization for Standardization/International
Electrotechnical Commission (2018) *ISO/IEC 14888-3:2018 −
Information technology − Security techniques − Digital signatures
with appendix − Part 3: Discrete logarithm-based mechanisms* (ISO,
Geneva, Switzerland). Available at
https://www.iso.org/standard/76382.html

      *This standard includes DSA as specified for finite fields and elliptic
curves in FIPS 186.*

ISO/IEC 18033-3   International Organization for Standardization/International
Electrotechnical Commission (2010) *ISO/IEC 18033-3:2010 −
Information technology − Security techniques − Encryption
algorithms − Part 3: Block ciphers* (ISO, Geneva, Switzerland).
Available at
https://www.iso.org/standard/54531.html

      *This standard includes 64-bit block ciphers (e.g., TDEA) and 128-
bit block ciphers (e.g., AES). Note that TDEA is specified in SP 800-
67, and AES is specified in FIPS 197.*

ISO/IEC 19772   International Organization for Standardization/International
Electrotechnical Commission (2009) *ISO/IEC 19772:2009 −
Information technology − Security techniques − Authenticated
encryption* (ISO, Geneva, Switzerland). Available at
https://www.iso.org/standard/46345.html

      *This standard includes CCM (as specified in SP 800-38C), GCM (as
specified in SP 800-38D), and key wrapping (as specified in SP 800-
38E).*

PKCS 1   Moriarty K (ed.), Kaliski B, Jonsson J, Rusch A (2016) PKCS #1: RSA
Cryptography Specifications Version 2.2. (Internet Engineering Task
Force (IETF)), IETF Request for Comments (RFC) 8017.
https://doi.org/10.17487/RFC8017

*PKCS 1 provides recommendations for the implementation of
public-key cryptography based on the RSA algorithm, covering
cryptographic primitives, encryption schemes, signature schemes
with appendix, and the ASN.1 syntax for representing keys and
identifying the schemes.*

RFC 3526   Kivinen T, Kojo M (2003) More Modular Exponential (MODP)
Diffie–Hellman Groups for Internet Key Exchange (IKE). (Internet
Engineering Task Force (IETF) Network Working Group), IETF
Request for Comments (RFC) 3526.
https://doi.org/10.17487/RFC3526

*This document defines new Modular Exponential (MODP) Groups
for the Internet Key Exchange (IKE) protocol.*

RFC 5288   Salowey J, Choudhury A, McGrew D (2008) AES Galois Counter
Mode (GCM) Cipher Suites for TLS. (Internet Engineering Task Force
(IETF) Network Working Group), IETF Request for Comments (RFC)
5288.
https://doi.org/10.17487/RFC5288

*This RFC describes the use of the Advanced Encryption Standard
(AES) in Galois/Counter Mode (GCM) as a Transport Layer
Security (TLS) authenticated encryption operation.*

RFC 7919   Gillmor D (2016) Negotiated Finite Field Diffie–Hellman Ephemeral
Parameters for Transport Layer Security (TLS). (Internet Engineering
Task Force (IETF)), IETF Request for Comments (RFC) 7919.
https://doi.org/10.17487/RFC7919

*This document establishes finite field DH parameters with known
structure.*

RFC 8017   *RSA Cryptography Specifications Version 2.2*, Internet Engineering
Task Force, Network Working Group, Informational RFC 8017, The
Internet Society; November 2016.
https://tools.ietf.org/html/rfc8017

*This document provides recommendations for the implementation of
public-key cryptography based on the RSA algorithm, covering
cryptographic primitives, encryption schemes, signature schemes
with appendix, and ASN.1 syntax for representing keys and for
identifying the schemes.*

RFC 8032   Josefsson S, Liusvaara I (2017) Edwards Curve Digital Signature
Algorithm (EdDSA). (Internet Research Task Force (IRTF)), Request
for Comments (RFC) 8032.

https://doi.org/10.17487/RFC8032

This document describes the Edwards-curve Digital Signature Algorithm (EdDSA).

X9.62   Accredited Standards Committee X9 (2005) *Public Key Cryptography for the Financial Services Industry: The Elliptic Curve Digital Signature Algorithm (ECDSA).* (American National Standards Institute), American National Standard for Financial Services (ANS) X9.62-2005. Available at https://webstore.ansi.org/SDO/X9

ANS X9.62 defines methods for digital signature (signature) generation and verification for the protection of messages and data using the Elliptic Curve Digital Signature Algorithm (ECDSA).

https://doi.org/10.17487/RFC8032

Appendix A: Revisions

In 2020, the following changes were made to the original (2015) version of this document.

1. Section 1.1: An alternative term, "integrity verification," was added to bullet 1, and a bullet for "Identity authentication" was added.

2. Section 1.5: Changes were made to the following terms: authentication, compromise, confidentiality, keying material, mode of operation, plaintext, secret key, source authentication, symmetric key, symmetric-key (secret) algorithm.

   The following terms were added: data-integrity authentication, domain parameters, identity authentication, integrity authentication, key confirmation, key information, key wrapping, metadata, owner of a certificate, owner of a key or key pair, pre-shared key, protocol, scheme, security function, server.

3. Section 1.6: The following acronyms were added: KMAC, OMB, ROTs, TPM.

4. Section 1.7: The summary of Section 4 was changed.

5. Section 2.2.3: A sentence was added about the prohibition of waivers.

6. Section 2.3.4: The dates from the list of ISO Standards were removed.

7. Section 3.1: SP 800-185 was added to the list of documents containing approved hash functions. Text was added to explain the nomenclature for the SHA functions and a bullet for SP 800-185.

8. Section 3.2.1.2: This section was revised to agree with the strategy for deprecating and/or disallowing the use of 2-key and 3-key TDEA.

9. Section 3.2.1.4: Text was added to explain the nomenclature used for AES and its acceptability.

10. Section 3.2.1.5: Paragraph 1 was revised to explain why modes are needed.

11. Section 3.2.2: A paragraph was added about SP 800-185.

12. Section 3.3: The text about the use of asymmetric-key algorithms was revised, and a note as added about post-quantum algorithms and why they are needed in the future.

13. Section 3.3.1: A general discussion of digital signature algorithms was added.

14. Section 3.3.1.1: Text was added to indicate that approval for DSA has been proposed to FIPS 186-5.

15. Section 3.3.1.2: Text was inserted that indicates that the elliptic curves will be provided in SP 800-186 rather than in FIPS 186. The last paragraph about the contents of the revision of FIPS 186 was changed.

16. Section 3.3.1.3: A new section was added about EdDSA which is specified in the latest revision of FIPS 186.

17. Section 3.3.1.4: This section has been revised to discuss RSA for digital signatures and to be consistent with FIPS 186-5.

18. Section 3.3.2: New introductory material on key-establishment schemes has been added.

19. Section 3.3.2.1: This section has been revised to include additional guidance on the use of domain parameters.

20. Section 3.3.2.2: Material from Section 3.3 of the previous version was added to specifically discuss the use of RSA for key establishment.

21. Section 3.4: Text was added to the end of the third paragraph about accepting the risks of using keys that provide only 80 bits of security.

22. Section 4.1: A sentence was added at the end of paragraph 1 that warns the reader about the deprecation of three-key TDEA.

23. Section 4.2: Text about the use of integrity codes was added at the end of the first paragraph. A paragraph about identity authentication was inserted, and the paragraph about source authentication was revised.

24. Section 4.2.2: This section on MAC algorithms was revised and reorganized.

25. Section 4.2.2.2: A paragraph was added about SP 800-185.

26. Section 4.2.3: The steps describing the generation and verification of digital signatures was revised (for easier understanding). EdDSA was added to the list of algorithms provided in FIPS 186-5.

27. Section 4.3.paragraph 2, was revised to include a recommendation to use well-vetted protocols and constructions.

28. Section 4.4: The description of SP 800-90B was revised.

29. Section 4.5: The third paragraph was revised to discuss key distribution. Text was added to the end of the last paragraph warning about the advent of quantum computing.

30. Section 5.0: An explanation of the term "key information" as used in the document was added.

31. Section 5.1.1: The description of the contents of SP 800-57, Part 2 was revised. A note was added that TLS is now discussed in SP 800-52.

32. Section 5.1.2: A new link to the CMVP was provided.

33. Section 5.2.3: EdDSA was added to the list of approved digital-signature algorithms. A discussion of the use of public keys, relying parties, etc. (above the bulleted items) was revised.

34. Section 5.2.3.1, item 4: A recommendation for the inventory of all certificates was added. A discussion of certificate expiration was expanded.

35. Section 5.3.2: The last paragraph was revised to indicate that the KDFs that were previously in SP 800-56A and SP 800-56B are now all in SP 800-56C.

36. Section 5.3.2.2: The material in Section 6.5 of the original version of SP 800-175B was inserted into this section.

37. Section 5.3.3, paragraph 2: Text was added to indicate that all key-derivation methods for SP 800-56A and SP 800-56B are now in SP 800-56C.

38. Section 5.3.4: The description of SP 800-56B has been changed, and a reference to SP 800-71 has been added.

39. Section 5.3.4.1: The first paragraph has been shortened.

40. Section 5.3.4.2: This is a new section about SP 800-71.

41. Section5.4.1: A reference to SP 800-71 has been added.

42. Section 5.4.5: The links to the CAVP and CMVP have been updated.

43. Section 5.4.8: This section has been revised to include both accountability and key and certificate inventory management.

44. Section 5.4.9: This is a new section on the different kinds of auditing.

45. Sections 6.4 and 6.5 have been removed.

46. The references have been updated.

NISTIR 7298
Revision 3

Glossary of Key Information Security Terms

Celia Paulsen
Robert Byers

National Institute of Standards and Technology
U.S. Department of Commerce

NISTIR 7298
Revision 3

Glossary of Key Information Security Terms

Celia Paulsen
Robert Byers
Computer Security Division
Information Technology Laboratory

July 2019

U.S. Department of Commerce
Wilbur L. Ross, Jr., Secretary

National Institute of Standards and Technology
Walter Copan, NIST Director and Under Secretary of Commerce for Standards and Technology

National Institute of Standards and Technology Interagency or Internal Report 7298 Revision 3
11 pages (July 2019)

This publication is available free of charge from:
https://doi.org/10.6028/NIST.IR.7298r3

Comments on this publication may be submitted to:

National Institute of Standards and Technology
Attn: Computer Security Division, Information Technology Laboratory
100 Bureau Drive (Mail Stop 8930) Gaithersburg, MD 20899-8930
Email: secglossary@nist.gov

All comments are subject to release under the Freedom of Information Act (FOIA).

Reports on Computer Systems Technology

The Information Technology Laboratory (ITL) at the National Institute of Standards and Technology (NIST) promotes the U.S. economy and public welfare by providing technical leadership for the Nation's measurement and standards infrastructure. ITL develops tests, test methods, reference data, proof of concept implementations, and technical analyses to advance the development and productive use of information technology. ITL's responsibilities include the development of management, administrative, technical, and physical standards and guidelines for the cost-effective security and privacy of other than national security-related information in federal information systems.

Abstract

This publication describes an online glossary of terms used in National Institute of Standards and Technology (NIST) and Committee on National Security Systems (CNSS) publications. This glossary utilizes a database of terms extracted from NIST Federal Information Processing Standard Publications (FIPS), the NIST Special Publication (SP) 800 series, select NIST Interagency or Internal Reports (NISTIRs), and from the Committee for National Security Systems Instruction 4009 (CNSSI-4009).

Keywords

cybersecurity; definitions; glossary; information assurance; information security; terminology.

Supplemental Content

The online glossary described in this publication is publicly available at
https://csrc.nist.gov/glossary.

Table of Contents

1   Introduction

The National Institute of Standards and Technology (NIST) has created an easily-accessible repository of terms and definitions extracted verbatim from NIST Federal Information Processing Standard Publications (FIPS), NIST Special Publications (SPs), and select NIST Internal or Interagency Reports (IRs), as well as from the Committee on National Security Systems Instruction 4009 (CNSSI-4009).

This repository ("the Glossary") contains two main parts: an online user interface application and an underlying database. The database, used as the foundation for the online application, contains terms and definitions extracted verbatim from NIST FIPS, SPs, and IRs, as well as from CNSSI-4009. The online application was developed to allow users to search the database of terms and definitions.

The Glossary is intended to help users understand terminology, recognize when and where multiple definitions may exist, and identify a definition that they can use. Over time, use of this Glossary will help standardize terms and definitions used, reducing confusion and the tendency to create unique definitions for different situations.

This publication provides a broad overview of the Glossary's design. It describes the methodology, assumptions, and constraints used in the development of the underlying database and associated online user interface application (available at https://csrc.nist.gov/glossary).   Specific implementation details are out of scope of this publication.

This publication differs significantly from previous versions of NIST IR 7298. Previous versions contained a subset of basic terms that were most frequently used in NIST publications. This method was valuable, but greater demand and frequent updates to NIST's publication suite has necessitated the adoption of a more flexible solution.

The audience for this publication also significantly differs from previous versions of NIST IR 7298. While the audience for previous versions included any reader interested in terms and definitions used by NIST, this publication is for a technical audience interested in the structure of the Glossary with its database and associated application, or anyone interested in learning about the purpose of the Glossary and decisions made regarding its development. Readers interested only in terms and definitions contained in the Glossary are encouraged to go to the online application at https://csrc.nist.gov/glossary.

2   Methodology

The Glossary contains two main parts: an online user interface application and an underlying database. The database, used as the foundation for the online application, contains terms and definitions extracted verbatim from NIST FIPS, SPs, and IRs, as well as from CNSSI-4009. This database will be updated regularly to accommodate new or updated NIST publications. The database may also be expanded to include withdrawn publications and relevant terms in external or supplemental sources, such as applicable laws and regulations. Recommendations for publications to be included in the database can be sent to secglossary@nist.gov. The database does not contain definitions without a source publication. Since draft documents are not stable, the database will not include their terms or definitions.

The online user interface application was developed to allow users to search the database of terms and definitions. It resides within the Computer Security Resource Center (CSRC) website[1] and will be updated as necessary to improve functionality and usability.

2.1   Database Structure

The Glossary uses a relational database to store and organize terms, definitions, and their associated sources. A relational database is used to provide a structured, consistent, and durable schema. The database is designed to allow for the following assumptions:

(1) A term may be related to one or more other terms. Terms may be considered identical but differ due to misspellings, alternative spellings, or abbreviations. These can be combined under a single "parent term".

(2) A term-abbreviation, -synonym, or other related pair may be associated with a source.

(3) A term may have one or more definitions.

(4) A definition defines one or more terms.

(5) A term-definition pair is associated with a source.

(6) A source may adapt or copy a term-definition pair from a referenced source.

Figure 1 shows a basic entity-relationship diagram of the database, excluding attributes or relationship types, with numbers corresponding to the above assumptions.

---

[1] https://csrc.nist.gov

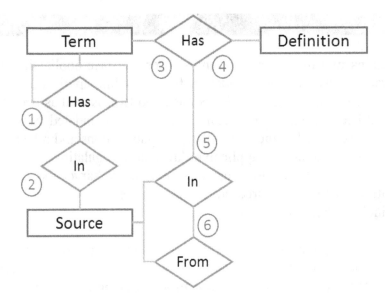

Figure 1: A basic Entity-Relationship diagram for the glossary database

2.2   Data

The glossaries, acronym lists, and equation lists of CNSSI-4009 and NIST FIPS, SPs, and IRs related to cybersecurity, information security or privacy are taken verbatim from their source and entered into the database. If a publication has no glossary, it is manually skimmed for terms explicitly defined within the text of the publication.

Because the Glossary is meant to reflect definitions published by NIST and CNSSI 4009, the relevant information is copied into the database as-is, meaning any errors (e.g., misspellings) in the publications are carried through into the database. The only times the text is altered from the original is when the definition includes a reference (e.g., "as defined in [1]"), in which case the reference is spelled out (e.g., "as defined in NIST SP 800-53"), when possible.

Terms that are referenced in NIST publications using various spellings or abbreviations (e.g., "control" vs. "controls") are identified and linked to a *parent term* (e.g., "control(s)"). These parent terms may or may not be used in NIST publications, however, they are used in the online application to group like terms together. Besides these parent terms, the database does not currently contain terms or definitions that do not have a source NIST or CNSS publication. On occasion, NIST receives a request to define a term: these requests are forwarded to authors responsible for publishing content related to that term. They may choose to define the term in a publication, in which case it will be included in the glossary database.

The database may have more than one definition for a single term. This occurs for many reasons: definitions can evolve over time, a broad definition may be tailored to a specific subject area, an existing definition may be altered to fit a unique topic, or there could be errors. In some cases, there may be definitions for a term that are very similar, yet subtly different, for example only differences in punctuation. These multiple definitions are preserved verbatum in order to precisely reflect the definitions in the publications and preserve the reliability and correctness of the Glossary.

Some definitions may have more "weight" or are more broadly recognized than others, definitions are prioritized by assigning each definition's source to one of these ranked categories (the lower the number, the higher the rank of the publication)[2, 3]:

(1) The definition is quoted (i.e., not adapted) from a federal law or regulation.

(2) The definition is quoted from an international, federal, or widely adopted technical standard [e.g., International Organization for Standardization (ISO), FIPS, American National Standards Institute (ANSI)], a common English or mathematical dictionary, or is an authoritative original technical source (e.g., the Defense Discovery Metadata Specification for the definition of the Defense Discovery Metadata Standard).

(3) The definition is quoted from an Office of Management and Budget (OMB) Policy or Circular, CNSS Policies and Directives, or similar documents.

(4) The definition is from NIST SPs, CNSS Instructions, OMB Memorandum, similar documents, or a specialized dictionary.

(5) The definition is from Government Accountability Office (GAO) Reports, CNSS Advisory Memoranda, Agency-specific standards, regulations, and policies.

(6) The definition is from NIST IRs, white papers, academic or technical papers, or other publications.

(7) The definition is from draft, archived, or superseded publications.

This ranking is not intended to reflect the importance of a publication or definition, but rather is intended as a means to describe the authoritative status of a definition from a general U.S. Federal Government agency point of view. The online application uses these rankings to determine the display order of definitions.

2.3   Web Application

The online application was developed to allow users to search the database of terms and definitions. It is expected that users will typically use the application in order to either (1) gain a better understanding of a term, or (2) find a definition to use. It will be regularly updated to improve functionality and usability based on user feedback.

The application was designed to be visually similar to other web pages on the NIST Computer Security Resource Center (CSRC) website[4], and attempts to provide as much relevant information as possible to the user. This means that the application may, for example, state that there are no

---

[2] Definitions that are "adapted" from another source are considered unique and the referenced source is not considered in this ranking. However, if there is no indication that the definition is adapted or altered from the referenced source, then the referenced source is considered. For example, if a NIST IR uses a definition from an international standards body, it will be listed under category 2 unless the NIST IR states that the definition is adapted, in which case it will be listed under category 6.

[3] A source may reference multiple other sources for a definition or may fit multiple categories; in these cases, the highest ranked category is assigned.

[4] https://csrc.nist.gov.

known acronyms for a term (instead of hiding that field). Because there may be multiple definitions for a term that are very similar, there may be increased complexity and confusion. It may become necessary to add functionality to the online application to limit searches to only those that are current (i.e., not withdrawn or superceded) or from higher-ranked category sources (e.g., categories 1 and 2 only).

The application is hosted at https://csrc.nist.gov/glossary.

3   Feedback & Updates

The glossary database will be regularly updated as new publications are finalized. Archived publications or publications from other sources (e.g., laws or standards) may be added. Recommendations for publications to be included in the database can be sent to secglossary@nist.gov.

Existing database entries will rarely be modified. Any change to a NIST document results in a new source—identified by a separate revision number or a new publication date—which would create a new source in the database; thus the change would be treated as a new addition. The old publication and associated definitions will not be removed, but will be marked as superseded or withdrawn, as appropriate. This will enable users to track changes to terms and definitions over time. Two exceptions to this rule are:

- when an error is identified and corrected; and
- when previously unknown information is added.

Occasionally, it is unclear what version of a document a term originates from (i.e., a referenced source). For these situations, the entry references a source with "unknown" information. This entry may be modified if the exact referenced source later becomes known. The database does not contain definitions without a source publication. Since draft documents are not stable, the database will not include terms/definitions from them.

The application may be updated frequently depending on user feedback. Users are encouraged to provide feedback on the usability of the application and/or if they identify any bugs in the application. Users are also encouraged to notify NIST of any errors in the glossary database, especially instances where the glossary does not match the term/definition in the associated publication.

Users may provide feedback using the email address provided on the web application. Feedback on the definitions themselves will be forwarded to the author of the publication source. Requests for adding terms to define will be sent to appropriate NIST subject-matter experts for consideration in future publications.

www.ingramcontent.com/pod-product-compliance
Lightning Source LLC
Chambersburg PA
CBHW060452060326
40689CB00020B/4499